POVERTY and POLITICS in HA

Report on Project Upli

POVERTY and POLITICS
in HARLEM

Report on Project Uplift 1965

BY

ALPHONSO PINKNEY
Hunter College

AND

ROGER R. WOOCK
University of Calgary

COLLEGE & UNIVERSITY PRESS · *Publishers*

NEW HAVEN, CONN.

606546

MANUFACTURED IN THE UNITED STATES OF AMERICA BY
UNITED PRINTING SERVICES, INC.
NEW HAVEN, CONN.

TO THE PEOPLE
OF HARLEM

Preface

This book is offered to the reader as a case study in the decline and fall of what has been known as the "war on poverty." The authors are well aware that American society in 1970 is quite different than it was on that spring day more than five years ago when Project Uplift was launched. Among the most important social changes that have occurred in the last five years have been:

1) the election of Richard Milhaus Nixon as President of the United States and the advent of a Republican administration. Although it is still too early to tell with absolute certainty what the effect of this Republican administration will be on poverty in the United States, there are ominous indications. Mr. Nixon's appeal to middle-class and especially southern white voters, his attempt to capitalize on the growing white backlash among working-class whites, and his apparent acceptance of advice from his chief urban affairs advisor, Patrick J. Moynihan, to treat the problem of urban blacks with "benign neglect," all suggest that the current administration has abandoned to a great extent both the rhetoric and the genuine attempts at reform of the two previous Democratic administrations.

2) the decline and collapse of the Office of Economic Opportunity. This office was created after the Economic Opportunity Act of 1964 with a tremendous amount of enthusiasm and idealism. A great number of young creative, if somewhat naive, men and women joined the OEO and for several years, at least, were able to be free-wheeling and cut through much of the red

tape which has historically stifled other federal programs. Many of the OEO programs (such as Headstart, and Manpower Training and Development) have been transferred to more traditional federal bureaucracies. The senior officials in the Department of Health, Education and Welfare and the Department of Labor have by now almost completely won the war against the upstart agency and what are left of its "boy wonders."

3) the rise of black power and black militancy in general. In part a response to the failure of moderate approaches to social change and to a growing realization of the structural social injustice in American society, black militants have been insisting in louder voices and with more direct action that they mean to control their own lives and develop their own institutions. The uprisings of summer 1967, although in no way organized or directed by black militants, nevertheless indicated clearly the inherent structural weaknesses in urban American society.

4) the growing radicalization of the young. Closely connected with the rise of black power is the increasing militancy of the young, both black and white, in American society. Bombing corporation headquarters and burning banks to the ground are new and very threatening attacks on the fabric of American society.

The above four developments and many more that could be enumerated suggest a society that is quite different from the one which the planners, organizers and administrators of Project Uplift faced in 1965. In that summer the "war on poverty" was a new and meaningful slogan, the federal government seemed concerned, the administration of the city of New York seemed at least sympathetically neutral, and all things seemed possible. It is the main thesis of this book, however, that the seeds for the 1965-1970 changes were in effect planted by programs like Project Uplift, and the struggles and failures of that program and others like it paved the way for the growing social chaos which characterizes American society today.

In the conclusion to *A Relevant War Against Poverty* Kenneth Clark and Jeannette Hopkins view the history of the "war on poverty." "It is reasonable to speculate that the frustrations of disadvantaged peoples are increased when verbal promises are not followed within a reasonable time by observable positive changes. These programs have made promises they have so far not been able to fulfill. The available evidence strongly suggests that they are not likely to be able to fulfill these promises. The failure of the community action phase of the anti-poverty programs as presently constituted has contributed significantly to the fuel of urban conflagration, increased the power of demagogues, and added to the restlessness, the alienation, and the sense of hopelessness of the deprived. Such ingredients make for profound social instability. Serious and considered analysis of the data of this study lead to the inescapable conclusion that only the development of an empathic, identified, independent coalition of trained, intelligent, committed professionals and the poor can increase the chances of a successful war against poverty and reduce the chances of social chaos. Yet even such a coalition must function in light of the probability that deprivation in many areas, such as education and employment, may not be responsive to programs of amelioration and community action. The problems of poverty cannot be resolved as if they were isolated from the wider economic, social and political patterns of the nation."*

To which the authors of this book would add that the coalition between professionals and the poor had better be under the direction of the poor in their communities. Clark and Hopkins, however, fail to deal with the most important question; namely, does American society have the political will to alter its social structure in a way which will not only alleviate poverty but bring the poor, all members of minority groups, and disaffected youth into some kind of relationship with the larger society? At this writing the prospects are certainly not good.

*   *   *

A large number of people have provided invaluable assistance in the preparation of this volume. First we wish to acknowledge our debt to all of the staff members, field workers, and young-

---

*Kenneth Clark and Jeannette Hopkins, *A Relevant War Against Poverty* (New York: Harper Torchbooks, 1970), pp.255-256.

sters involved in Project Uplift. Of special assistance were members of the evaluation section, particularly the office manager, Mrs. Madeline Monroe, and the executive secretary, Mrs. Phyllis Scott. Frank Stanley, the director for most of the life of the project, was particularly helpful both during the summer and at a later date when he read and made contributions to several chapters. Robert W. C. Brown of International Research Associates contributed greatly to collecting the research on which much of this study is based.

Alphonso Pinkney
Roger R. Woock

Contents

CHAPTER ONE

Introduction

Why the "War on Poverty"?

In the second half of the twentieth century Americans have suddenly discovered the millions of poor people living in the richest country in human history, at a time of unparalleled affluence. To quote former President Johnson in one of his State of the Union messages: "Our nation's industries, shops and farms prosper today far beyond the dreams of any people, any time, anywhere." It is as if these unfortunates suddenly descended upon this richly endowed land. Widespread poverty is therefore viewed by Americans as an unexpected phenomenon rather than the logical consequence of certain economic and social arrangements and practices.

The present concern with the elimination of poverty in the United States represents a reversal in thinking about social problems. Poverty has always existed in the United States, and there have always been attempts on the part of humanitarian social reformers to deal with it. There have even been large scale governmental programs designed to assist the poor: for example, the New Deal. Frequently these programs have succeeded in raising the standard of living for those whom Gunnar Myrdal calls the "underclass." But the poor continue to reappear on the scene.

The question must then be asked: Why the need for the so-called "war on poverty" in the seventh decade of the twentieth century? Many factors account for the continued existence of millions of poor people in the United States. One of the most salient factors is what might be called assumptions characterizing American attitudes toward poverty and the poor. Through the years, a set of assumptions regarding the relations between citizens, the role of government toward citizens, and the relations of citizens to the productive processes have developed. These assumptions have frequently become institutionalized in the culture to the extent that they have become part of what is frequently referred to as the "American way of life." The following are a few of these assumptions relevant to the question posed above:

1) *The notion of rugged individualism.* The feeling that an individual's destiny is to be determined by him alone has permeated American thinking since the first Europeans settled on this continent. It is assumed that through hard work one is destined to succeed in achieving a standard of living comparable with the level of technological development of the society. If for some reason the person fails to achieve this, it is generally considered desirable to assist this "unfortunate," but programs of massive social and economic reform have never been seriously considered. The "individualistic" approach to social problems may succeed in preventing certain individuals from starving or suffering from malnutrition, but it fails to get at the source of the problem by denying the social basis of poverty.

2) *The absence of social justice as a value.* While humanitarianism is clearly an American social value, the notion of social justice has never been widely shared in the United States. This is, of course, a logical outgrowth of the notion of rugged individualism. The concern of the society has tended to center on individual unfortunates rather than on instituting programs which would insure a more equitable sharing of the social rewards of the society. Many modern nation-states strive toward the equal sharing of such social rewards as employment, education, medical care, and housing. In contrast, the United States has tended to emphasize those values which have come to be known as individual "liberties" or "freedoms"—freedom of speech, freedom of assembly, freedom of religion, and freedom to change one's place of residence.

3) *The sacredness of private charity.* Publicly sponsored programs to deal with problems of poverty have always been met

with hostility or at least suspicion in the United States because it was feared that they would ultimately lead to socialism, and capitalism as an economic system has been and is still considered infallible. Public programs are felt to stifle individual initiative. For example, the Chamber of Commerce of the United States proposed to the Congress that a significant segment of the anti-poverty program—adult education and retraining—be sponsored by private foundations as a means of curbing the "growing scope of government in American life." Although private charity has succeeded in dealing with some cases of destitution, it has rarely dealt with the large masses of people who are not destitute but who suffer from poverty.

4) *The inevitability of poverty.* The assumption that any citizen who tries can somehow "get ahead" is a long standing myth in American society. Failure to achieve "success," the supreme social value, simply indicates a lack of initiative. Therefore, those people who are poor suffer this misfortune because they lack the initiative to "get ahead." They do not continue trying again and again after failing to succeed. A certain proportion of the citizenry is assumed to lack aspirations to the degree necessary for financial success. Hence, "the poor we shall always have with us." Clearly, if a condition is defined as inevitable, an attitude of hopelessness develops in relation to it and little effort is exerted to remedy the condition.

5) *Concern with the economy rather than with people.* Historically, the concern and policies of the national government in relation to poverty have been directed more to the needs of the productive processes than to the needs of people. Poverty is seen as an enemy of the productive system. The trouble with poor people is that they are too numerous, and their chief fault is that they do not buy enough. Living in a society with a proliferation of consumer goods, everyone must want and need to purchase these products. Therefore, the problem is to increase the productive capacity of the economy. If the needs of the individual and the productive capacity of the society could somehow be synchronized, production and purchasing power would then be brought into a working relationship. Hence, the prevention of poverty appears to be a problem of economic necessity rather than one of social justice.

6) *Poor people enjoy their poverty*. It is often felt that those people who receive some form of public assistance do so because in this way they can evade the task of providing for themselves. That is, they enjoy receiving hand-outs. This notion has led to numerous punitive welfare laws in municipalities and states throughout the country. An increasing proportion of citizens on welfare rolls is seen as an indication that somehow many people would prefer receiving a one-hundred dollar monthly check rather than, say, three-hundred dollars monthly from productive employment. Social workers frequently comment about welfare clients who sit at home surrounded by material possessions and await welfare checks. In other words, those people who depend in part or in full on public assistance are simply parasites who enjoy their condition. Hence, slogans such as "I fight poverty—I work" are seen increasingly on automobile bumper stickers by those opposed to anti-poverty programs.

7) *Concern with pauperism rather than with poverty*. One of the proudest achievements of American society is the virtual elimination of starvation in the United States. Unlike most of the "underdeveloped" world, starvation and malnutrition have never really been major social problems in the United States. The major concern of many welfare officials has been more maintenance at a subsistence level, for a significant proportion of citizens, rather than insuring a standard of living compatible with the level of technological development of the society. In general, social reformers have been interested in those people who find themselves in a state of total dependence on either public welfare or private charity. In recent years, however, the focus has changed and some concern has developed for those who have not yet become totally dependent.

8) *Simplistic view of social problems*. Since social problems are not generally seen as social in origin, rarely are they approached logically. Usually they are viewed as individual problems without social bases. The task, then, is to rehabilitate the individual rather than to attack the problem at its source. Numerous individual researchers, voluntary associations, private foundations, municipal, state and federal commissions have been appointed, especially in the twentieth century, to investigate problems of poverty, but rarely are their recommendations acted

upon by administrators or legislators. In general, the American approach to social problems is that they can be solved without basic social changes. The approach is a cautious one, and every effort is made to avoid the possibility of upsetting those in positions of power whose main interest is maintaining the status quo.

It is clear that many of these assumptions are overlapping. However, they have been dealt with separately because each contains elements independent of the others which can be separated out for purposes of discussion. Also, it must be admitted that some of these assumptions are less deeply rooted today than they were at previous periods in American history. Rugged individualism, for example, was less pervasive as a value in the 1960's than it was in the 1860's. The same is true of the notion that poverty is inevitable. However, these notions have made their impact on American culture and are likely to continue to characterize the thinking of a significant proportion of citizens.

Whether or not the present efforts will succeed in significantly affecting the condition of poverty in the United States remains to be seen. Clearly, how much will be accomplished depends on approaching the problem logically and seriously. The climate of opinion in the late 1960's appeared to be favorable for a concerted attack on the problem. A significant segment of the population indicated a willingness to take whatever measures are necessary in order to provide a decent standard of living for all Americans. For example, the Ad Hoc Committee on the Triple Revolution urges that "society, through its appropriate legal and governmental institutions, undertake an unqualified commitment to provide every individual and every family with an adequate income as a matter of right." In other words an American citizen is entitled to live decently whether or not he is employed.

Others have advocated the adoption of some type of family allowance system as practiced in western European countries. Still others have advocated a negative income tax. These are but a few of the far-reaching proposals advanced as a result of the unprecedented concern about the poor.

Changes in ways of perceiving problems and of dealing with problems come slowly, and rarely keep pace with developments in technology. It is one thing to "declare war on poverty," and quite another to deal effectively with it as a social problem. The assumption must be made, however, that poverty amidst afflu- ence is a social creation and is therefore amenable to a social solution.

What This Book Is About

The purpose of the present volume is two-fold. First, the authors believe that an examination of Project Uplift (PUL), the Harlem summer 1965 crash project funded by the Office of Economic Opportunity and the City of New York, is important to readers concerned with ameliorating poverty in America. Har- lem is, after all, perhaps the most crucial black community in the United States and no major federal effort to deal with its problems, however brief or inadequate, is without interest.

There is no doubt in the authors' minds, however, that the importance of PUL, its successes and failures, extends far be- yond the project itself and even beyond future projects in Harlem. Questions are raised in this volume concerning the fund- ing, planning, execution, and evaluating of poverty programs that have implications for all future programs and, in fact, for the direction and nature of the struggle against poverty itself. Quite aware of the danger of glib generalizations drawn from a single case, the authors have guarded against this danger in the text. This volume will be useful as a handbook of what to do and what not to do in similar projects.

The plan, then, is to present the reader with a case study of one large, short-term poverty program in a single community and then offer criticisms, comments, suggestions, and programs cast in the broader context of the "war on poverty."

Harlem was the setting for Project Uplift. Although perhaps more has been written about Harlem than any other black com- munity in America, a description of it is essential for under- standing the successes and failures of PUL, as well as other efforts which have been made in this community. Life in Harlem is described including figures on unemployment, housing con- ditions, crime rate, and infant mortality, realizing that these figures cannot adequately convey the frustration and despair they only hint at. The young people of Harlem must be of particular concern since PUL was designed to serve them and since the failure of public education in Harlem is notorious. (In a later chapter the authors deal specifically with the young people directly involved in PUL.) Some comparisons are made with other communities to show in what particular ways (e.g., absentee ownership of property) Harlem is unique. Finally, the concepts of subculture and slum mentality are treated briefly, indicating the impact of these concepts on the life of Harlem residents.

Quite frequently in published reports on government projects the planning and development phase of the project is ignored. This is particularly unfortunate since many failures and serious problems can be traced to this early period. This was clearly the case with PUL. In Chapter III the development of the project is traced from the first ideas of the Urban League for a "clean-up Harlem" campaign through the negotiations with Harlem Youth Opportunities Unlimited (HARYOU) and its designation as the prime contracting agency. Also examined are the early relations with the Office of Economic Opportunity and the city poverty office; the crucial change of PUL to the status of "demonstration project"; and the role of political figures both local and national in planning and implementing the project. Of considerable importance for the final results were the project's original objectives and their modifications during the planning phase. In Chapter III are also described the design of the project, the structure of relationships between the project and its parent organization HARYOU, as well as the four prime sub-contractors, Associated Community Teams, The Urban League of Greater New York, Harlem Neighborhood Association, and Harlem Administrative Committee. Also discussed are the delays in release of funds and the introduction of new programs and activities while the project was in operation. Some of these additional programs proved to be either particularly successful (e.g., the final Parade and Festival) or controversial (e.g., The Black Arts Theatre).

A universal problem in "crash" programs of any kind is the selection and recruitment of an adequate staff to effectively carry out the stated goals. Chapter IV looks carefully at the selection criteria established for PUL and their application. It became necessary in certain areas, for example, to recruit outside of central Harlem because essential skills were not available. One objective of PUL was to raise the skill level of staff members while they were on the job. In a program involving thousands of youth and hundreds of staff members this goal, however worthy, meant serious difficulties in the smooth functioning of various programs. Considerable publicity in the New York press about PUL was generated by the resignation of the project co-ordinator. The authors felt obligated to deal with this situation in as objective and dispassionate a manner as possible and hope that the discussion may help to clear up any confusion surrounding this series of events. Since the staff of Project Uplift worked for a variety of local community' organizations as well as the central project staff, these inter-relationships are examined as well as relationships with the permanent staff of the parent organization, HARYOU.

The purpose of PUL was to usefully employ, train, and educate a large number of youth from central Harlem. How were they recruited and what was the nature of the work they accomplished during the summer? Chapter V looks directly at this most important aspect of the project. A number of special problems related to the "enrollees" became apparent as the project developed during the summer. The period between intake and assignment to a specific work task was important. From the enrollees' point of view the question of pay, particularly receiving it on time, became a crucial problem. The enrollee is portrayed as he appeared during the summer project. What was his self-image? With which groups and individuals did he identify? What was his social and economic background? And how did the project itself affect this picture? Finally, a day's experience for a "typical" enrollee is presented.

One of the most delicate aspects of any program in a slum is the program's relationship to the community at large. Chapter VI considers the ways in which PUL made itself known to the Harlem community via its own newspaper, press releases, radio and television interviews with project staff and mass media coverage of its major activities. How aware were members of the Harlem community of PUL's existence and of the nature of its activities? Closely related is the identification of PUL as a separate project in relation to HARYOU, the on-going permanent social agency in the Harlem community. A number of special public activities were sponsored during the summer including the Harlem Olympics for young athletes, the Black Arts Theatre which performed on streets throughout central Harlem, and the final Parade and Festival in Central Park to which all participants as well as Harlem residents were invited. These public activities and the attempts to encourage media coverage of PUL activities raise the general question of public relations as an aspect of poverty projects. Chapter VI attempts to establish the need for some kinds of "public relations" while pointing out important dangers in publicly financed programs engaging in the activity of selling themselves to local communities.

Having examined the planning and organization, the staff, the youth, and the relationship of PUL with the Harlem community, what must the authors conclude about the accomplishments and failures of this crash program? Chapter VII points to some clear accomplishments. It is a fact that the program did provide employment for large numbers of young people and adults in central Harlem; that it did strengthen group identification for some enrollees; that in certain specific areas, notably the summer day camps and building repair crews, the work done by the youth was of very high quality. On the other hand, a number of areas must not be overlooked in which the project clearly failed to measure up to either the initial design of the proposal or to what could reasonably be expected as the summer progressed. Some failures can be directly traced to the lack of lead time provided during the planning stage. Other problems of major proportion were the handling of funds, resulting in delays of payment for the enrollees, and supplies and equipment not arriving at work sites when needed. It also became quickly apparent that some work programs were ill-conceived from the beginning and could not reasonably have been expected to succeed in a crash program. The design of the tree planting program failed to take into account the fact that summer is the worst time for transplanting trees and that there was a serious water shortage in New York during 1965. A stumbling block also arose with city ordinances and planting permits. The result was that one (instead of 1500) tree was planted. In Chapter VII the authors also identify those components that would be particularly useful to other poverty programs, other summer projects, and other slum areas in the United States.

The authors of this volume believe that the analysis would not be complete if it did not go beyond either describing or criticizing programs which have been implemented thus far. Chapter VIII makes suggestions and recommendations for programs which the authors believe to be essential for fundamental change and improvement in Harlem. There is no doubt in the authors' minds that both long range massive and comprehensive programs are necessary in many areas if the lives of Harlem residents are to be fundamentally altered. Many suggestions and recommendations have been made by other writers, such as massive job training and employment programs, greatly improved schools in central Harlem, and urban renewal projects for improving living conditions. There is a great need to develop programs specifically designed to foster the development of grassroots leadership.

Harlem is, of course, not the only depressed community in the United States and along some dimensions of poverty it is not the worst. The struggle against poverty has many battlefields. The authors believe, however, that what can be learned from an examination of this project and what should be done for Harlem will have many points of relevance for poverty programs in other communities across the country.

The main focus of Chapter VIII is the amelioration of poverty in urban black communities through change in the areas of economic development, political development, and education. The local control of economic, political and educational institutions is projected as a first step in this direction.

CHAPTER TWO

Harlem: The Setting

Historical Development

At the turn of the present century Harlem was a secluded upper-middle-class, white residential community. There were few blacks, other than domestic servants, to be found there. It was the home of some of America's best known and wealthiest families. Today, in a relatively short period of time, the community has been transformed into a massive black community, and the name itself is synonymous with the characteristics of its residents, both the color of their skins and the stereotypes which have developed about them through the years. It is known the world over as the largest and most densely populated single concentration of black people anywhere. European tourists coming to the United States are eager to see one of New York's most publicized neighborhoods, and native white New Yorkers rarely go to Harlem because they fear physical violence will meet them on its streets. White social workers assigned to the area refuse to visit their clients unless accompanied by another person. Teachers in Harlem's elementary and junior high schools eagerly await the sound of the closing bell and flee to the "safer" sections of the city, breathing a sigh of relief that they "made it" through the day without being attacked. White policemen patrol its streets in constant fear, often having been sent there as a form of punishment for offenses committed in other precincts. Merchants anxiously await the close of the business day when they can fortify their shops with iron bars and rush off to the safety of the all-white suburbs. In many of these regards Harlem is strikingly like an occupied colonial territory.

The events responsible for the development of this community are many. Some of the factors motivating migrants from the south to settle in Harlem are not unlike those which gave impetus to immigrants from Europe to settle in the United States. At the turn of the century uncontrolled violence directed toward southern blacks was rampant. Hence, during the first two decades of the century thousands of them came up the eastern seaboard and settled in New York. Like European immigrants, these migrants settled with relatives or at least in neighborhoods with those with whom they shared some common characteristics. But unlike immigrants from Europe, black migrants, because they were black, could not lose their characteristics and move out of the slums. They were rarely afforded the opportunity to advance themselves economically or educationally, and those who were able to "make it" were still hampered by the badge of inferiority—their inherited physical characteristics.

In addition to escaping violence from southern racists, thousands of blacks migrated to New York for economic reasons. While they could not expect to earn salaries comparable to those of white New Yorkers, they could count on earning substantially more than they were paid in southern agriculture. With the outbreak of World War I, the migration to New York to work in war plants and related industries was widespread. This was at a time when the steady flow of labor from Europe had been greatly curtailed. Representatives of northern industries traveled throughout the south recruiting black workers. Most of the blacks coming to New York settled in Harlem, and during the first two decades of the twentieth century Harlem developed into a predominately black community.

Blacks living on Manhattan Island have not always lived in Harlem. They moved in stages from the southern tip of the island northward to Harlem, but wherever they lived, they were forced to concentrate in neighborhoods with other blacks. The movement northward to Harlem gained impetus with the massive riot of 1900 when blacks were brutalized by citizens and police alike. This riot occurred in a section of mid-town Manhattan known as the Tenderloin. It erupted when a black man killed a plainclothes policeman. It remains one of the most brutal of those characteristically American patterns of racial adjustment.

Not only did the police not protect the blacks from mobs of whites, they joined the mob. With this outbreak, the blacks in New York realized that they could not expect to live peacefully in neighborhoods with white New Yorkers. Hence, they moved north to Harlem at the first opportunity, seeking peace with their neighbors.

The blacks who lived elsewhere in New York had been living in squalor, and because Harlem was a spacious community with attractive rows of well-designed houses, it was only natural that they would take advantage of the opportunity to acquire desirable living quarters when the subway line was extended northward. As the white residents of the community moved out, as is so characteristic of American urban racial patterns, the blacks moved in. The demand for adequate housing on the part of blacks afforded real estate speculators an opportunity to charge rentals far in excess of the going rate for comparable living quarters elsewhere in the city.

The proportion of black residents in the population of Harlem continued to increase for the first half of the century, when it became almost solidly black. As is usually the case, living areas open to blacks are limited, and they are forced to live where they can. That Harlem remains a black community simply reflects a continuing pattern of discrimination. That it contains such a large number of blacks is a function of such historical factors as attempts to flee physical violence and terror, and the search for greater economic opportunities.

Population Characteristics

With each census since the turn of the century the proportion of Harlem residents who are black has increased, reaching a peak of some 98.2 per cent in 1950. In 1960 the census recorded some 7,781,984 residents in New York City. Of this number, 1,087,931 were entered as black. The Borough of Manhattan housed some 1,698,281 people of which 397,101 were black. What is defined as Central Harlem (to distinguish it from East Harlem which is predominantly Puerto Rican) housed some 199,637 residents, including 193,800 blacks.

As these figures indicate, the proportion of Harlem residents who are black declined (from 98.2 per cent) to 97.0 per cent between 1950 and 1960, mainly as a result of low-income Puerto Rican families moving into public housing developments in the area. Manhattan houses more than one-fifth of New York's residents, and nearly two-fifths of New York's blacks. Harlem houses slightly more than one-tenth of Manhattan's residents, and 97 per cent of Manhattan's blacks.

The 193,800 inhabitants of Harlem live crowded into a mere three and one-half square miles, making it one of the most congested areas in all of the western world. In density, this means more than 100 people per acre, and more than 50,000 people per square mile. Within this land area, a small proportion of the land (roughly ten per cent) consists of public parks, compared to the rest of the Borough in which more than sixteen per cent of the land is devoted to public parks.

Harlem is a community of young people. According to the census of 1960, nearly one-third of all of its residents are under 20 years of age, and another two-fifths are under forty-five. These figures are strikingly like those of the underdeveloped countries of the world where recent improvements in health and medical care have served to curb the incidence of infant mortality, thereby making for significant proportions of the population in the dependent-child category.

Furthermore, Harlem as a community has an unbalanced sex-ratio. Females predominate. For every forty-five males in the area there are fifty-five females. The sex-ratio is unbalanced at all age levels, with males predominating at all levels through the teens, when females begin to predominate. This suggests that upon reaching adulthood, males move out of Harlem, leaving females behind.

The economic conditions of the community affect the patterns of family formation in Harlem. This is reflected in the proportion of residents separated from their spouses. About three times as many Harlem residents are separated from their spouses as is the case in the Borough of Manhattan in general. The number of separated individuals is significantly greater for females than for males (30 per cent and 19 per cent, respectively).

Harlem has a significantly higher proportion of individuals not living in families than does the Borough of Manhattan. Nearly one-fourth of the individuals live outside of families in Harlem, compared with ten per cent for Manhattan. Furthermore, within Harlem households four times as many families report relatives other than members of the nuclear family (husband, wife and children) in residence than is true of the Borough of Manhattan.

The average family size in Harlem, however, is not significantly greater than that in New York City as a whole. There are 3.27 persons per family in Harlem, and 2.69 per family in New York City.

Housing

Harlem is primarily a residential area. There are fewer commercial and industrial establishments compared to other sections of Manhattan. Over two-thirds of the land is devoted to housing. There are 87,000 dwelling units in the area, and while Harlem, compared to Manhattan, has many public housing projects, most of the buildings are dilapidated. A vast majority of the buildings are more than thirty-five years old, built to provide emergency housing for the influx of immigrants from southern and eastern Europe. As a matter of fact, nearly one-half of the multiple dwelling units were constructed before the turn of the present century.

The census of 1960 reports that only one-half (51 per cent) of the housing units in Harlem are sound, while half are either "deteriorating" or "dilapidated." (The figures for New York City as a whole are 85 per cent sound and 15 per cent either "deteriorating" or "dilapidated.")

In addition to the unsafe and unsanitary physical condition of housing units in Harlem, they are vastly overcrowded. Nearly one-fifth of all housing units contain more than one person per room, while the figure for the City of New York as a whole is a mere twelve per cent.

Nine giant public housing developments in or bordering on Harlem provided some relief from overcrowding and substandard housing. As of 1964, these developments contained 10,349 apartments with 47,288 rooms, and accommodated 41,120 inhabitants. Another seven developments were under construction or in the planning stages. These new developments provide 2,196 apartments for 8,895 additional residents.

Not all of Harlem consists of either substandard housing or public housing. In addition to privately owned single-family dwelling units such as the elegant and spacious brownstones designed by Stanford White on "Strivers Row" (139th Street between Seventh and Eighth Avenues), there are six large middle-income housing developments containing some 7,751 apartments. The over-all picture, however, is one of too many people living in dwelling units which do not provide either adequate or safe shelter. As a rule, few of the housing units in Harlem are owned by residents. Rather, they are generally owned by absentee landlords who make no attempt to maintain their upkeep.

Occupations and Employment

Harlem has few large businesses. There are many small commercial enterprises, however. One survey identified some 1,617 commercial enterprises, consisting mainly of those in the food and beverages industries such as bakeries, catering houses, grocery stores, liquor stores, luncheonettes, restaurants, bars and taverns. More than one third (or 565) fall within this category. The next largest category (27 per cent) of businesses is those engaged in personal services such as barber shops, beauty parlors, and dry cleaning establishments. The next most frequently found businesses are stationery stores (136), furniture stores (70), insurance companies and agencies (69), pharmacies (67), funeral homes (63), jewelry stores (32), and employment agencies (20) which usually specialize in domestic help. The business establishments in Harlem are usually owned and operated by white, non-residents of the community.

Among self-employed professionals, Harlem has 130 medical doctors, 125 lawyers, and 90 dentists.

In 1960, a vast majority of the residents of Harlem were employed in low status occupations. For example, of the residents of Harlem who are employed, less than four per cent were employed in a professional capacity, while one-third were employed as service or domestic workers. In many ways, as has been true historically, the black female fares better than the male. There are twice as many female professional workers living in Harlem as male professional workers. This reflects the historical pattern of black women working as nurses, teachers, and social workers.

In addition to working in low status occupations residents of Harlem eligible for the labor force are at least twice as likely to be unemployed as are white residents of New York City. Again, Harlem is like colonial territory. If one drives through the streets of Harlem at, say, eleven o'clock in the morning or three o'clock in the afternoon on a regular work day, one sees many able bodied men standing on street corners. In non-slum areas this phenomenon is absent because jobs are available. The unemployment rate for Central Harlem has not dropped below eight per cent in the last fifteen years. Among the younger workers, the unemployment rate reaches 50 per cent at times. And at no time in the last twelve to fifteen years, has the unemployment rate dropped to a figure of less than double the rate of unemployment among white workers.

Low status occupations, underemployment and unemployment are reflected in earnings. The median family income in Harlem in 1960 was $4,021 compared to $5,338 for New York City as a whole. Half of the families of Harlem have incomes of $3,000 or less, compared to one-third of the families in New York City, and only four per cent have incomes exceeding $10,000, while one-fifth of all families in New York City have incomes in this range. Furthermore, studies show that the income gap between blacks and whites is widening rather than narrowing.

Individual incomes for residents of Harlem are, on the average, lower when compared to other residents of New York City. In 1960, the median income for Harlem residents was about 60 per cent of the median for the city. This reflects the general American pattern in which blacks with the same educational qualifications as white Americans can expect to earn in their lifetime slightly more than half as much as their white counterparts.

Community Pathologies

As is suggested by the preceding statistics, Harlem is a community of pathologies. It would indeed be rare for a people to live within the harsh atmosphere described above without such social conditions resulting. These conditions affect the citizens at birth and continue throughout their lives.

The birth rate for Harlem is higher than the city as a whole just as is the rate for blacks in the United States higher than the national average. For every 1,000 residents in Harlem there were 25.4 live births in 1962, compared to 21.2 for New York City as a whole. The death rate is 13.2 per 1,000 citizens compared to 11.2 for New York City. In both of these cases, Harlem is strikingly like the underdeveloped world, and in terms of its death rate, it is significantly higher in the most advanced city in the country with the most highly developed technology in all of human history, than in many of the underdeveloped countries. The black baby born in Harlem stands slightly more than half as much chance of surviving infancy as a white baby born elsewhere in New York City. The infant mortality rate for Harlem is 49.5 per 1,000 live births, compared to 27.3 for New York City as a whole.

And so it is with death from communicable diseases. One of the proudest achievements of mankind is the control over death resulting from diseases which a few decades ago decimated whole populations. The United States has historically been a leader in the control of these diseases. Much of the medical technology for their control was developed in this country. Yet, in many regards, blacks lag behind white Americans. The incidence of tuberculosis serves to illustrate the point.

In 1963, one-fourth of all reported active cases of tuberculosis in Manhattan were among residents of Harlem, while they made up only about one-tenth of the population. A significant proportion of these cases recover, but among those who die, one out of every three is a resident of Harlem. At the present level of technological development in the United States, the death rate has declined radically for diseases easily controlled by modern medicine. Today Americans die from such morbid conditions as cancer and heart diseases. That blacks have continued to die of controllable diseases is a serious indictment of society.

The adverse living conditions affect not only the physical health of Harlem residents, but their social behavior as well. The area is well known for its disproportionately high rates of juvenile delinquency, narcotics addiction, and venereal disease. These are frequently viewed as resulting from the moral character of the residents of Harlem rather than from the type of lives they are forced to live.

The crime rate in general, and the juvenile delinquency rate in particular, have reportedly been on the increase in the United States for some time. The same pattern has been reported for Harlem's juvenile population. In 1953, for example, the number of crimes committed by youth between seven and twenty years of age per 1,000 people in the population was 36.2. This rate increased each year and reached 68.5 in 1962. In New York City the rates showed comparable increases; that is, in New York City as well as in Harlem the rates doubled, but in each year Harlem's rates were significantly higher. The New York City rate increased from 23.3 in 1953 to 47.0 in 1962.

The habitual use of narcotics in Harlem is widespread. As in the case with juvenile delinquency the rate of narcotics usage has increased through the years. It is frequently reported that more than half of the narcotics addicts in the United States live in New York City and that there is a high proportion of non-white (mainly black) users of narcotics. The New York City Department of Health reports that in 1961, for example, there were slightly more than 4,000 habitual narcotics users in New York City, while Harlem alone accounted for nearly 1,000 of these; that is, fully one-fourth of the reported habitual users of narcotics in the city were black. It is quite likely that in both the case of New York City and Central Harlem the rates reported represent an underenumeration because the criminal provisions accompanying such use, of necessity force secrecy around such acts. Regardless of the inaccuracy of the statistics reported to the Department of Health, Central Harlem is plagued by narcotics. Sample surveys conducted among its residents invariably report that widespread and increasing use of narcotics is one of their greatest concerns.

The incidence of venereal disease is reported to be on the increase among youth through the United States. As with juvenile delinquency and narcotics addiction, Harlem again stands out with one of the highest rates of venereal disease in the city. In fact, the rate for Central Harlem is six times that of the city as a whole. The New York City Youth Board reported that

among young people under twenty-one years of age, about one-
fifth of all cases of venereal disease were reported among Harlem
youth.

Education

For the last several years education has been the single most
controversial issue in Harlem. As an area, Harlem is not lacking
in the number of schools within its boundaries. At the present
time there are fourteen public elementary schools, three public
junior high schools, one "twenty-first century intermediate"
school, two private high schools, and six Roman Catholic paro-
chial schools in Harlem proper. Two well-known high schools,
one catering to the intellectually gifted student, are on the edges
of the area.

The controversy, however, has stemmed mainly from the educational achievement of Harlem youth. The ethnic composition
of the more than 32,000 Harlem school children is considered to
be the key to the relatively low achievement levels of these
students. In the elementary schools, in 1962, ninety per cent of
the students were black, nine per cent were Puerto Rican, and
one per cent were classified as other, which for the Board of
Education means that they were white. In junior high schools,
there were nearly 96 per cent blacks, nearly four per cent
Puerto Ricans, and fewer than one per cent whites. The ethnic
composition of all schools was 91 per cent black, nearly eight
per cent Puerto Rican, and slightly more than one per cent
white. Harlem parents and civil rights organizations maintain
that the absence of white pupils in the schools results in the
virtual refusal of teachers (who are mainly white) to teach these
pupils adequately. Other factors, they say, such as the widespread practice of using substitute teachers and poor physical
facilities simply compound the problem.

Whatever the cause, and a significant proportion of the responsibility must rest with the teachers and administrators, the
educational achievement of Harlem students lags behind students
in the city as a whole. Such a situation begins in elementary
school and is compounded as they pass up the educational
ladder. There is a steady deterioration in pupil performance
from elementary school through high school as measured by

standard educational tests utilized in the public schools of New York City. For example, on three of these tests—reading comprehension, word knowledge, and arithmetic—such a deterioration is reported. In third grade, Central Harlem students perform relatively low on both reading knowledge and word comprehension, as many as two-fifths (depending on the school) of them reading below grade level. By the time they reach sixth grade, as many as ninety per cent may read below grade level.

On arithmetic tests, anywhere from one-third to four-fifths of sixth graders perform below grade level. In general, about 75 per cent of Harlem pupils score below grade level in both reading comprehension and word knowledge, and in arithmetic the figure exceeds 80 per cent. Inasmuch as there is a steady deterioration as they go through school, the parents appear to be justified in charging the teachers with failure to teach the students adequately. Also, there is a consistent decline in performance on intelligence tests as these students "progress" through school.

The performance of these students in junior high school affects the type of curriculum which they will pursue in high school. At a far greater rate than is true for students in general these students are sent to vocational high schools or enrolled in vocational curricula in the standard high schools. All of this means that when it is time to enter college (should they reach this point), the likelihood is that they will not have maintained the required average or perform well enough on the examination to gain entrance into college. Such a situation is manifest by the proportionately few non-white students attending the tuition free municipal colleges in the City of New York prior to the end of the 1960's.

A disproportionately large number of Harlem youth never complete high school. That is, they are drop-outs. A survey of the graduates of junior high schools in the area in 1959 reports that of those who went on to high school, more than half dropped out before graduation. In the academic high schools, 53 per cent of the students did not graduate while in the vocational high schools the figure climbed to 61 per cent. This is in contrast to the over-all drop-out rate of about ten per cent for the city as a whole.

In general, youth from Central Harlem are less inclined than other youth in New York City to remain in school. But a more serious indictment of the schools in this area is the tendency for these students to lag behind other students in New York and in the country as a whole in educational achievement. Early in their school careers these students perform less well than others and as they continue through school the gap widens. For example, at the third grade level they are about one year behind the achievement levels of other New York students, and by the time they reach the eighth grade they are more than two-and-one-half years behind. Most observers concede that Harlem youth perform poorly in school. Differences appear, however, on the source of the problem. Educators place the blame on the home life of the youth, while the parents blame the teachers for failing to teach their children properly. The educators call for cultural enrichment programs while the parents call for better teaching which they say is only likely to be achieved with community control of the schools.

Opinions of Residents

What do the people of Harlem think? Self-styled leaders frequently make pronouncements on this question without consulting those for whom they presume to speak. Rarely are the people given an opportunity to express themselves. In a survey, conducted in 1964, blacks throughout New York City were asked to express themselves on a variety of issues—educational, economic, and social—affecting their lives. While Harlem was just one of the many areas studied, wherever black people live in New York they share many common problems. The responses they gave give some idea of their aspirations for their children and for themselves. Responses to such questions are necessarily complex because these people are living in the most complex city in what is in many ways the most complex country in the world. But through the responses one gets a picture of the hopes and aspirations of a people struggling to improve their lives and those of their children.

Economic problems overshadow most of the other many problems of the black people in New York and those in Harlem, in particular. And these economic problems have many facets. The first is, of course, the necessity for employment. Unemployment in Harlem remains at least twice the rate for New York City as a whole, and for the young adults the differential is even greater. Many explanations are offered for the abnormally high unemployment rates among Harlem's residents, but these people understand that their economic problems in general stem from the same source as their other problems—their being black. The charge is frequently made that they are unable to secure employment because of lack of skills. At the same time, they are not given the opportunity to develop the appropriate skills. Discriminatory practices on the part of business and labor unions operate in such a way that blacks find it impossible to improve themselves.

When they finally secure a job, as most of them ultimately manage to do, they can expect to earn a fraction of what white workers earn, even when employed at the same levels. Blacks in Harlem still tend to be concentrated in the lowest level jobs in both government and industry. These low status jobs provide but a fraction of the income necessary to maintain an adequate standard of living in New York City. Therefore, they find it necessary to accept subsidies in order to maintain themselves and their families. It is little wonder that economic problems overshadow all others for Harlem's residents.

Following economic problems, the residents of Harlem list housing as a major problem. The housing problem, too, has many facets. In the first place they complain about the condition of the housing units in which they are forced to live. All too often they are forced to live in unsafe and unsanitary conditions which they share with rats and roaches. Most of the units contain many violations—the plumbing does not work, they are without heat and hot water in winter, the plaster falls down, etc. In general, they are forced to live in housing which does not meet the minimum health and safety standards. In addition, the housing units are overcrowded. There are too many people per room. Privacy, in the sense that most Americans have come to expect, is minimal. Needless to say, this in itself leads to other problems. There is inadequate space for children to study, and the sleeping arrangements are such that a comfortable night's sleep is for many of them a rarity. For these conditions it is often required that the residents of Harlem pay rents far out of proportion to the worth of the living units. Rental rates per square foot of floor space in Harlem are among the highest in New York City.

The adverse economic and housing conditions in Harlem are direct contributors to the third major problem voiced by its residents—crime. Some observers find a contradiction in the charges of police brutality by blacks in Harlem, and their constant requests for greater police protection. But the evidence is overwhelming that an oppressed people are frequently extremely aggressive toward one another. Oppression and constant submission to a superior power may cause a people to brutalize others like themselves. In Harlem, as in other Harlems throughout the country, crimes against persons are widespread. Hospitals are at their busiest after the weekend disorders. Muggings and stabbings are so frequent that residents are often afraid to leave their apartments at night. Crimes against property are also widespread in such areas. Breaking and entering forces many residents to live in terror. Apartments are frequently secured to the extent that they resemble maximum security prisons.

Other crimes like the sale of drugs and the numbers racket are widespread, and the residents know that these acts frequently exist with the full knowledge and approval of the police. It is mainly for the sake of their children that the people of Harlem express so much apprehension about the widespread practices of these acts. The youth learn at early ages that through these acts they can achieve status which has been denied them by the more conventional, socially acceptable channels.

A fourth major concern of Harlemites, and one which appears to be increasing in importance, is the education of their children. From bitter experience these parents have arrived at the conclusion that the present educational set-up is such that the low educational achievement level of these students is perpetuated. They see the solution to the problem as one of greater community control over the local schools or racial integration in schools. It is their contention that white teachers in the schools simply do not teach their children unless they are in classrooms with white students. They do not view integration as an end in itself but rather as a means toward achieving better education for their children. Since integrating children from Harlem would require sending these children long distances, many of them reject this notion. (Nevertheless, in 1964 a plurality of them expressed favorable attitudes toward school busing.) Opposition to busing appears to be on the increase since it involves many practical problems. The parents are now calling for greater control over the schools. They want more black teachers and administrators in the schools of Harlem, and greater emphasis on Afro-American and African history and culture in the curriculum. Most of all they express a desire for teachers who are seriously concerned with the education of their children. Whether this can be accomplished with more black teachers and administrators remains to be seen, but the parents feel that the situation at the present time is such that while it may not improve the situation, conditions could hardly get worse. Aside from the lack of interest on the part of teachers, the parents cite the following as the major problems in the schools: overcrowding, causing double shifts and split sessions; lack of cooperation from parents; unsanitary conditions; poor materials—books, paper, etc.; poor administration, including insufficient preparation on the part of teachers.

In addition to the four major problems cited above, the blacks interviewed listed several others. Among them were 1) indifference and apathy on the part of blacks themselves, including the refusal to fight for reforms necessary to improve the condition of their lives; 2) the lack of concern which they feel that many black parents manifest toward their children; 3) prejudice and discrimination directed toward them by whites in New York.

This survey investigated the attitudes and opinions of blacks on a variety of issues, ranging from their feelings about white Americans to attitudes toward non-violence as a technique for meeting the problems which they face as blacks in American society. An overwhelming majority of them report that their feelings about whites are neutral—that is, they neither hate nor like them. It is inevitable that there is hatred by some blacks toward whites, but it is nothing short of remarkable that a people who have so often been brutalized by another can maintain neutral rather than negative feelings toward them. All surveys show that blacks in the United States have consistently less hostility toward whites than whites have toward blacks.

On the question of black leadership, a vast majority of them expressed a preference for Martin Luther King, Jr., as the leader who was doing the best job. He was followed by Roy Wilkins of the NAACP, and Adam Clayton Powell, in that order. No other leader was selected by more than eight per cent of those questioned. Of interest in their expressed preferences for leaders is a clear-cut preference for leaders who have come to be identified as moderates in the civil rights movement, with their elected congressional representative, Adam Clayton Powell, as a possible exception. Few of them selected such acknowledged militant leaders as Malcolm X, Jesse Gray, or Milton Galamison.

Again, when asked which of the civil rights organizations was doing most for blacks, they tended to choose the less militant organizations. More than half of them selected the National Association for the Advancement of Colored People (NAACP), and while one-fifth selected the Congress of Racial Equality (CORE), a somewhat militant direct action group, this was followed by the most conservative of all the groups, the Urban League. Both the Southern Christian Leadership Conference, and the Student Nonviolent Coordinating Committee received few endorsements because at the time these groups were active mainly in the South. The Muslims, and such social service agencies as HARYOU and Associated Community Teams were named by few people as making the greatest contribution to the civil rights movement.

Inasmuch as there was overwhelming endorsement of Martin Luther King, Jr., as the most effective leader, and the NAACP as the most effective organization, it follows that these residents would endorse the policy of non-violence as the approach most likely to succeed in achieving equal rights. Nearly two-thirds of them reported that they approved of non-violence. A significant proportion said that although they disapproved of violence, they felt that it was inevitable.

In the responses given to a variety of questions, one gets the impression of a people struggling to improve themselves within the context of the society in which they find themselves. They disapprove of separation from whites—most of them approve of school integration for their children, and few (10 per cent) express a preference for living in all-black neighborhoods. Their aspirations are probably not unlike those of most Americans. That is, they are interested in the best possible life for themselves and their children.

Summary

Harlem, in the second half of the twentieth century, is a major depressed area in a country which is enjoying unparalleled economic prosperity. As one reads statistics on the major social problems plaguing this community, he cannot help being struck by the parallels which exist between this community and the so-called underdeveloped world. It is a powerless community, resembling a colonial territory. The major support for the community comes from outside sources; the economy is dominated by outsiders. Even the many small businesses which exist in the community are owned and operated, for the most part, by people who do not and would not live within its boundaries. The rows of inadequately maintained tenement houses are owned by affluent (and often politically prominent) suburban residents. Its schools are manned and controlled by outsiders. "Law and order" are maintained by a suspicious force of policemen who are not responsible to the people they are supposed to protect. In short, the residents of Harlem are, in almost every respect, subject to forces over which they have little or no control.

Again, like the peoples of the underdeveloped world, Harlem's residents are experiencing a high rate of fertility and a declining rate of mortality. They are high on rates of communicable diseases, and social pathologies are rampant. They are exploited in the labor market, and continue to provide a ready source of cheap labor. Their unemployment rate is more than twice the national average, and the rate of functional illiteracy is high. A significant proportion of the population is in the dependent-youth category. In fact, the parallels between Harlem and the underdeveloped world are so striking that one social critic has referred to this situation as a form of "internal imperialism."

Such a situation inevitably leads to massive social problems. To attribute all of the ills of this community to racial discrimination perhaps oversimplifies the problem. But it is not an oversimplification to say that an overwhelming majority of the problems which these citizens face stem from their being black in a racist society. It is nothing short of extreme irony that citizens can be forced to pay taxes and fight in wars by a government which assumes no responsibility for their earning a living or living wherever they can afford. It is axiomatic in the modern world that governments reserve for themselves a significant degree of control over the lives of citizens. This being the case, the conditions under which the citizens of Harlem live exist with the consent of government—federal, state, and municipal. More specifically, the problems of racial discrimination, the drug traffic and gambling about which so many Harlem parents complain, would not and could not exist without the knowledge and cooperation of the police in the area. Officials of government could insist that landlords maintain apartment houses in a manner suitable for human habitation if they chose to do so.

Historically, and up to the present time, Americans have made a point of enforcing their will on people the world over. They give the impression of assuming the role of policemen to people of the world. And in most cases they are efficient and powerful enough to do so. To say that the same could not be done on behalf of citizens in its midst is nothing short of absurd. Harlem and the many Harlems in America exist because they are permitted to do so.

A great deal is written about the police in Central Harlem. Charges of police brutality frequently generate unrest in the community. The police understandably deny that this phenomenon exists. Yet many people who have been arrested have been taken from the police station to the hospital on stretchers after having walked in. It is unlikely that a single citizen could create a situation in which it would be necessary to restrain him with such force as to require his hospitalization. But this is just one of the many problems faced by citizens who live in a system of internal imperialism. The general situation is such that their actions are understandable if not laudatory. How can citizens be expected to exemplify high standards of civic and social responsibility when they are continually denied the rights of citizenship which others enjoy simply by virtue of being white?

As a community Harlem is not devoid of social agencies. Religious organizations (there are more than 400 churches in Harlem), non-sectarian private organizations, and government agencies, representing the Federal government, the state and the city operate a variety of social services in Harlem. There are more than 100 playgrounds in the area. But these agencies fail to come to grips with the most pressing needs of the community—greater economic opportunity, better education, and adequate housing. Rather, they tend to focus their attention on recreational and child-care services as a means of keeping the youth off the streets.

In recent years cries of "black power" alarmed the nation. Some spokesmen in Harlem have been advocating the establishment of a separate nation in Harlem independent of the administrative structure of the City of New York. To many, perhaps most, such cries appear ridiculous. They are not really so far-fetched in the context of modern times when people the world over are demanding independence and self-determination. Harlem and its inhabitants are not unlike their counterparts in Africa, Asia, and Latin America in terms of their powerlessness.

Americans have never feared "power" until it was preceded by the word "black." Somehow the combination is more than they can take. They see it as black supremacy and black violence. Yet most of the white immigrant groups to the United States—the Irish, the Italians, the Jews—have been able to mobilize themselves into power blocs as a means of improving their status in the society. When interpreted objectively, the concept is a logical one meaning the growth of black political power, economic power, and consumer power. Furthermore, it means the development of positive identification among blacks. Given the history of the black man in America, black power is a logical and inevitable development. Too often blacks have been betrayed by white Americans in positions of power and their own leaders, and are angry. Such is the setting within which one of the first demonstration projects, funded by the Office of Economic Opportunity, would operate during the summer of 1965.

CHAPTER THREE

The Organization of Project Uplift

Background

On July 16, 1964, several black pupils who were on their way to summer school classes became involved in a dispute with a building superintendent. An off-duty white police lieutenant intervened and claimed that one of the pupils, a fifteen-year-old male, threatened him with a knife. He then shot and killed the teen-ager. A large crowd of other teen-agers appeared to protest the murder but they were dispersed by a force of hundreds of policemen. Several community groups in Harlem held meetings to protest the killing and leaflets charging police brutality saturated the community. At one of these meetings a march on the police station was organized. Once there, the demonstrators clashed with the police, who retaliated with force, killing one person. Altogether an additional nineteen citizens and twelve policemen were injured. For the next several days the residents of both Harlem and Bedford Stuyvesant "rioted" against police brutality. They looted stores and threw bricks and bottles at the police. The police responded with gunfire, and many hundreds of persons were injured. Following those in New York City, disturbances erupted in several other cities that summer: Rochester, New York; Jersey City, Elizabeth, and Paterson, New Jersey; Chicago; Philadelphia.

During the winter governmental officials at all levels discussed ways of preventing a repetition of the events of 1964. The major social agency in Harlem, Harlem Youth Opportunities Unlimited (HARYOU), had published the report of its eighteen-month study, "Youth in the Ghetto." This report set forth a program of change in Harlem through self-help in the areas of education, employment, the family, and community organizations. This report, more than any other document, served as a basis for discussions on how the residents of black communities might be motivated to engage in a series of projects aimed at reconstructing slum areas.

In March of 1965, the Executive Director of the National Urban League addressed a group of Harlem residents. In this speech he put forth a proposal for a summer clean-up campaign in Central Harlem. This proposal resulted from conferences in the Urban League designed to expose black youth throughout the country to meaningful and creative work experiences in their communities. These projects would serve the dual purposes of improving communities and channeling the energies of the youth into constructive areas. At the same time representatives of HARYOU were considering ways in which this organization could assist in the avoidance of summer disturbances by youth.

A United States Senator from New York learned of the proposals of the Urban League and HARYOU and sent a staff representative to meet with officials of both groups. In these discussions it was agreed that some type of summer project was necessary to prevent the youth of Central Harlem from "rioting" in the summer of 1965. It was also agreed that any large scale project would be co-sponsored by both HARYOU and the Urban League of Greater New York.

On April 19 staff members from the two organizations met to discuss and plan a summer project in Harlem called "Clean Up Harlem." The idea for a summer clean-up campaign had originated with the Urban League, but officials of HARYOU insisted that any program should be broader in scope, in keeping with the proposals contained in "Youth in the Ghetto." A compromise was reached in which the two organizations agreed to a plan for a large scale summer project in Harlem to involve thousands of youth working through already existing neighborhood organizations. The facilities of HARYOU would be utilized for recruitment and referral, while specific areas of control would be allocated to neighborhood organizations on a contractual basis. These agencies would administer programs in five general areas: physical environment, education, health and safety, recreation, and family life.

It was agreed that funding for the project would come directly from the newly created Office of Economic Opportunity (OEO) to HARYOU so that the people of the Harlem community would feel that the project was community-based rather than dominated by city officials. In May, at the request of the director of HARYOU, an official of the National Urban League was appointed coordinator of the proposed project. He was assigned office space in the building which housed the offices of HARYOU, the Hotel Theresa at 125th Street and Seventh Avenue, and a small staff was assembled to draft a proposal for the project. This proposal was based on the Community Action section of the Economic Opportunity Act of 1964 and submitted to Washington for funding in mid-May. Officials of OEO indicated a willingness to fund a summer program, but suggested that the proposal be. rewritten and submitted under a different section of the Act, making it a demonstration project. With the assistance of consultants from OEO, the staff redrafted the proposal during Memorial Day weekend and resubmitted it to Washington.

In the following weeks details of the program were clarified. The Neighborhood Youth Corps of the U. S. Department of Labor, which was administered locally by New York City's Economic Opportunity Office, was asked to assist in sponsoring and financing the program since this agency serviced sixteen to twenty-one-year-olds from poor neighborhoods, a major target population of the proposed summer project. Approval for the summer project was secured from the several city, state, and federal officials directly concerned with anti-poverty programs.

Inasmuch as OEO had expressed a willingness to fund the program, details of contractual arrangements with neighborhood organizations were worked out after the proposal was resubmitted. Staff and enrollees for the program were recruited, and administrative procedures were effected. In general, while awaiting final approval, the temporary staff attempted to make all arrangements necessary to start the program as soon as funding was approved. The funding was finally approved on June 25, 1965.

The Proposal

Project Uplift, according to the approved proposal, was designed to deal with four specific problem areas: 1) the problem of powerlessness in Central Harlem: an attempt was to be made to provide power to the poor; 2) the physical blight of the area: the reduction of squalor was seen as a means of developing a sense of pride in the community; 3) the lack of recreational activities: the proposal called for providing planned recreation as a means of developing cooperation and interdependence in children, and providing fatherless children with new role models; 4) the school drop-out problem: it was felt that a program of useful work and sympathetic guidance could have a positive effect on the attitudes of early adolescents toward education.

The proposal rested on four basic assumptions:

1. Concrete accomplishments will give purpose and power to neighborhood organizations.

2. The accomplishment of specific projects which meet expressed felt needs of concerned adults will increase the level of participation in neighborhood organizations.

3. The assignment of responsible roles and visibly useful tasks to unemployed youth will increase their self-concept and sense of identity. This will be particularly true when the task involves the giving of service to others.

4. Young people will more readily accept direction and help from their near-peers than from adult strangers.

The proposal stipulated that three groups of youth would be enrolled in the summer project:

1. Children between fourteen and sixteen years of age were to be employed as program aides. They were to work thirty-two hours weekly. Included in the thirty-two hours would be eight hours of educational, cultural, and counseling activities aimed at improving both academic aspirations and academic achievement.

2. Neighborhood youth aged sixteen to twenty-one were to be employed as staff assistants. They were to work forty hours weekly, eight of which should have an educational and guidance content.

3. Young adults, aged twenty-one to twenty-five were to be employed as full-time staff associates. Remedial education and

planning for the future were to be provided for these associates through staff seminars and in-service training activities.

In addition to serving the youth of Central Harlem, the proposal stipulated a variety of program vehicles designed to meet clearly defined community needs. These program vehicles fell into six general classifications:

1. To provide helping services to school age children through the day camp program, resident camps, organized sports, street work, child-care, and accelerated remedial reading.

2. To provide helping services to adults through information services, guided tours, and emergency homemaker services.

3. To provide increased recreational facilities such as vest-pocket parks and indoor play areas.

4. To reduce the squalor of slums by landscaping and tree planting, renovating community facilities, painting, decorating and beautifying.

5. To identify and train potential leaders and increase neighborhood participation by providing community workers and opinion survey teams.

6. To increase the skill and strength of neighborhood organizations by the managing of the summer project and planning for future projects.

The proposal stipulated that the summer project would be executed by several existing community organizations in Central Harlem. Four of the larger and more successful agencies would serve as prime contractors through which specific programs would be subcontracted to some eighty-nine neighborhood groups. The four contract agencies were to be the Associated Community Teams (ACT), the Harlem Administrative Committee (HAC), the Harlem Neighborhood Association (HANA), and the Urban League of Greater New York. ACT, which was established in 1962 and which had instituted programs for youth and adults in the area, would assume responsibility for the day camps and recreational programs. HAC, a newly formed group of ministers, was given responsibility for the public information and historical landmarks program, and for the emergency homemaker program. HANA, a community social service agency was to assume responsibility for the vest-pocket parks program. The

Urban League of Greater New York, the oldest of the contract agencies, would be responsible for beautification and tree planting.

The program components of Project Uplift and the agencies responsible for each of them as outlined in the proposal, included the following:

1. Central Administration
     Remedial Reading
     Community Surveys
     Neighborhood Development
2. Associated Community Teams
     Day Camps
     Resident Camps
     Athletic Workshops
3. Urban League
     Building Repairs
     Tree Planting
4. Harlem Administrative Committee
     Information Booths
     Historical Landmarks
     Emergency Homemaker Service
5. Harlem Neighborhood Association
     Vest-Pocket Parks

The Administrative Staff

Since HARYOU served as the applicant agency for the summer project, the Board of Directors of the agency assumed ultimate responsibility for setting policy. The line of authority for the program was as follows:

> Board of Directors of HARYOU
> Executive Director of HARYOU
> Associate Director of HARYOU
> The Coordinator and Staff of Project Uplift
> Contractors' Special Project Staff
> Subcontractors
> Enrollees

The central administrative staff was the core of the summer project. It made the accomplishments of the project possible, and it was also responsible for many of the shortcomings of the program. While HARYOU may have been ultimately responsible for setting policy, the central administrative staff of the project was responsible for its ultimate success or failure. It was organized into the following posts and departments:

1. Project Coordinator and his special assistants
2. Executive Assistant to the Project Coordinator
3. The Administrative Cabinet:
   a. Personnel
   b. Program Development and Training
   c. Job Development and Guidance
   d. Medical Office
   e. Supply Office
   f. Comptroller
   g. Legal Office
   h. Public Relations—Community Relations

The Project Coordinator and his special assistants, and the executive assistant to the Coordinator were responsible for the over-all operation of the project. A significant proportion of their time was spent in negotiations with city, state, and federal officials. Therefore, it was necessary for them to delegate responsibility for many aspects of the program to the "cabinet officers" as the key professional personnel became known. These persons comprised the administrative cabinet and their responsibilities will be enumerated below. Evaluation of how well they accomplished these tasks will be made in later chapters.

The Administrative Cabinet of the summer program consisted of people who were responsible for the day-to-day operations of the project. The Personnel Department had two major objectives: 1) to process enrollee applications as quickly as possible, and to assign the enrollees to contract agencies; and 2) to hire professional staff and supervisory personnel to work with the central administrative staff. The first task was assigned to the Youth Placement Division, while the second was assigned directly to the executive assistant of the Project Coordinator.

The objectives of the Program Development and Training Department were 1) to develop programs in day camps, 2) to organize and direct training of all professional staff and enrollees, 3) to organize and supervise the neighborhood training vehicle,

4) to maintain proper liaison with appropriate city agencies, 5) to act as liaison with contract agencies and subcontractors, and 6) to assume responsibility for the over-all quality of the entire project. These functions were not enumerated in the proposal, rather, they were the functions of this department as interpreted by its director.

No provision was made in the original proposal for dealing with what the enrollees would be doing at the end of the summer project. As the program developed this question was raised with increasing frequency, and the Project Coordinator and his staff created the Job Development and Guidance Department to meet this need. The stated objectives of this department were 1) to assist enrollees to return to high school and finish their secondary education, 2) to assist those enrollees who were qualified to enter college or to continue their college education, 3) to develop a scholarship fund to help prospective college students in need of financial assistance, 4) to discover as many full and part-time jobs as possible for enrollees attending both high school and college, 5) to compile a directory of other social agencies with job development units, and 6) to develop a test training program with particular emphasis on the Scholastic Aptitude Test.

The Medical Office's responsibility involved administering complete physical examinations to all enrollees in the program in keeping with city and state laws. A team of volunteer doctors and nurses made this task possible.

The Supply Office was created at the insistence of OEO. The primary function of this office was to facilitate and speed up the requisitioning, purchasing, and distributing of all furnishings, equipment, and supplies to the staff of central administration, contract agencies, and subcontract agencies. The office had no authority to initiate requests or authorize purchases of any supplies or materials. In addition to its primary function, this office also set up and operated a duplicating service for the entire project. Finally, this office was responsible for transportation services for the project, including the thirty-three floats used in the parade and festival at the end of summer.

The Comptroller's Office did not exist as a separate department of the summer project. Rather, the Comptroller's staff of

HARYOU was expanded and all purchasing and paying was funneled through that office. The original proposal called for a business manager, a position ultimately translated into supply expediter. An assistant comptroller was employed by the summer project. He interpreted his function as seeing that everyone in the project was paid on time, and all money was allocated in accordance with the budget as devised by OEO and the Neighborhood Youth Corps. In addition, this office purchased supplies and equipment, paid the bills for these items, rented office equipment and furniture, and automobiles.

The Legal Department was organized four weeks after the project was underway. Many of the tasks ultimately performed by this office were those which had accumulated in this period. The primary responsibility of this department was preparing and executing prime contracts between HARYOU and the principal contract agencies and the various neighborhood organizations. In addition, this department was charged with 1) advising all other departments on legal problems, 2) inspecting and advising all departments on contracts and supplies, 3) advising and transmitting all accident reports to insurers, 4) advising and transmitting all stolen property reports to insurers, 5) advising and transmitting all lost property reports to insurers, 6) preparing and supplying forms for reports of accidents, stolen property and lost property, 7) advising prime contractees and subcontractees on all legal problems, 8) inspecting installations of contractees and subcontractees, 9) inspecting programs of contractees and subcontractees, and 10) attending conferences, when requested, to supply legal advice.

No provision was made for the Public Relations-Community Relations Department in the initial proposal. As this department evolved, it centered on two main functions. First, the department was designed to instruct enrollees in the various communicative arts and crafts. It provided them with work-training experiences, giving those youth with no prior knowledge ideas about the techniques of communication such as booklets, pamphlets, and the spoken word. The second objective was to produce professional materials for distribution to residents of the Harlem community and the mass media. The activities of this department fell into six specific areas. A regular weekly eight-page newspaper, "Newsbriefs" was produced by the staff of this department. An art department was established to prepare visual materials: posters, leaflets, flyers, and the drawings which appeared in "Newsbriefs." A dance troupe, the La Roque Bey Dancers, was organized by this department. They performed several times during the summer. The Project Uplift Art Gallery, sponsored by this department, was designed to show the work of Harlem artists to the community. A public relations distribution unit was responsible for distributing all materials from the department, including "Newsbriefs" throughout the Harlem community. Finally, the department sponsored the community survey which was stipulated in the initial proposal. The objectives of this survey were the following: survey associates would be trained to identify neighborhood needs, evaluate the impact of the project on the community, and assist block and tenant organizations in the development and encouragement of maximum resident participation.

As the project developed it expanded on many fronts. Among the new activities added were the following: the youth congress, the final parade and festival, the Black Arts Repertory Theatre, the consumer research unit, the black heritage program, voter education and registration drives, the Harlem Olympics, and the Sunday Songfest.

Administrative Interrelations

In order to get the summer project underway, it was necessary to establish several departments and staff them in a rather short period of time. These departments and the hundreds of individuals staffing them were somehow expected to operate as a functioning unit for a period of ten weeks. Needless to say, friction between individuals in these departments developed as the project unfolded. As in any organization there was an interdependence, and frequently an overlapping, of functions. While many of the individuals who headed the various administrative departments had had prior experience in administration, some were novices. At the beginning, a spirit of comradeship and cooperation was apparent, but as time went by strain between various administrative officials developed. Some of the strain resulted from vaguely defined duties and responsibilities, and some of it resulted from personality conflicts. In general, however, those individuals who made up the administrative cabinet worked well together. The one glaring exception to this rule was that the director of Program Development and Training, for personality reasons, was unable to work with any other official in the project. Because of the strategic relevance of this department, the smooth functioning of the project was impossible.

Relations between project officials and those of the parent and sponsoring agency, HARYOU, too were frequently strained. The summer project's administrative offices were housed in the same building, the Hotel Theresa, as those of HARYOU. While there was little physical contact between the employees of the two groups since they were housed on different floors, summer project officials were dependent upon HARYOU officials in many ways. Perhaps the crucial area in this regard was in the office of the Comptroller. While an assistant comptroller was hired for the summer project, final authority rested with HARYOU's Comptroller. Unaccustomed to the volume of business which the summer project involved, the Comptroller's office was frequently unable to cope with it. Consequently, pay for summer employees and supplies were frequently delayed. While both of these were crucial functions in the summer project, the Comptroller's office handled such matters with undue casualness.

Furthermore, HARYOU was justifiably concerned about its image. It was a relatively new organization and was interested in establishing itself as one of the chief anti-poverty agencies in New York City. Consequently, its officials were anxious to see that whenever summer project press releases were issued, they should indicate that the project was sponsored by HARYOU. (No such problem arose with the New York Urban League because it was not the grantee-organization, and its offices were located several blocks away.)

In a few cases summer project personnel were made to feel that they were unwanted intruders at HARYOU. Life had been reasonably simple before the advent of the summer project, and although the project operated reasonably autonomously, the smooth functioning of HARYOU was seriously impaired by the addition of Project Uplift.

There was little contact between summer project officials and

those of the neighborhood organizations. While contracts between these groups and the prime contract agencies were drawn
up by the legal staff of Project Uplift, it was the responsibility
of the prime contract agencies to see that the terms of the
contracts were fulfilled. Officials from the central administration
did frequently visit these agencies in order to inspect their
programs.

The central administration did maintain close relations with
each of the four prime contract agencies. In most cases relations
were good, except when various officials from central administration visited these agencies with multiple, and often conflicting, requests. Frequently, officials in the prime contract
agencies expressed the feeling that their activities were being
endlessly policed.

The problem of image was of concern to these agencies. All
of them, except the Urban League of Greater New York, were
relatively new agencies and it was important that they convey a
favorable image to the Harlem community. Therefore, each of
them sought favorable publicity from the central administrative
staff.

In general, however, the relations between Project Uplift's
administrative staff and the staffs of the prime contract agencies
proceeded without friction throughout the summer. In most
cases these agencies hired special officials for their summer project activities.

Administrative Headquarters

Project Uplift's administrative staff was mainly housed in the
Hotel Theresa, an aging building which was in the process of
being converted into an office building. This had at one time
been Harlem's most expensive hotel, catering to black celebrities,
especially when it was likely that they would be denied accom-
modations at downtown hotels. Now, it was experiencing its
final days as a hotel. HARYOU had leased two floors as its
administrative headquarters, and since Project Uplift's staff was
to be larger than the permanent staff of HARYOU, three floors
were leased for the project.

These floors were entered through a service entrance with a
receptionist whose job it was to determine whether persons

attempting to gain entrance had legitimate reasons for being there. All who entered, except those whom the receptionist happened to know, which included few of the summer project personnel, were required to stop at the desk, state their business and the person they wished to visit. The receptionist then proceeded to telephone upstairs to find if the visitors should be sent up. For the personnel of the summer project this proved to be a long and frequently embarrassing procedure. Lengthy delays were avoided as the summer progressed because the receptionists gradually recognized Project Uplift employees.

The five floors leased by HARYOU and Project Uplift were serviced by a single manually operated service elevator. This was clearly inadequate for the hundreds of employees involved. Frequently the service of the elevator was required to transport office supplies and equipment, thereby forcing passengers to wait for long periods in the hot entrance foyer. In terms of the many problems which arose during the summer, elevator service was a relatively minor one, but it did have its effect on the morale of the employees of the central administration.

Once one went upstairs, the working space was adequate. Most of the offices of central administration were housed in suites of rooms which were air conditioned and which contained private bathrooms. The three floors proved to be adequate initially, but with the addition of new programs, lack of space became a problem.

That Project Uplift was able to be housed in Hotel Theresa on perhaps the busiest corner of Central Harlem was fortunate. Its very presence there served to bring it to the attention of the residents of this community in a way which would have been impossible had it been in a less visible location. Furthermore, being on a major intersection minimized food and transportation difficulties.

This brief description of the organization of Project Uplift is intended to convey some of the complexities involved in planning, staffing, and operating a large project in a major depressed area in a short period of time. Although there were many difficulties involved, as will be discussed in detail in later chapters, Project Uplift was able to function and did make some impact on the Harlem community. The primary objective of the project for politicians and other leaders was to forestall a repetition of what became known as the "riots" of 1964. Whether such a project, organized to operate for ten weeks, can have this effect is doubtful, but Harlem, like most other American cities, was relatively quiet during the summer of 1965. This presumably justified the expense from the politicians' point of view.

Many of the organizational difficulties of the project stemmed from its complex nature. It was sponsored by the two major social agencies in Harlem, and its operation depended upon close cooperation among four of the other social work agencies and nearly 100 neighborhood organizations. The over-all organization of Project Uplift was basically sound; whether a project organized in this manner is workable is the subject of the following chapters.

CHAPTER FOUR

People in the Project: Staff

A midway progress statement reported that the Project Uplift staff "has grown to 410 with varying professional disciplines and a high degree of professional competence." It continued, "Project Uplift has been able to attract to its integrated staff an impressive array of dedicated talent. Seven hold doctorates, two are lawyers, two [are] social psychologists, a number [are] civil rights organizers, statistical clerks, graduate students most of whom are indigenous to Harlem or residents of contiguous areas." As is generally true of reports of this kind, the competence and dedication of the staff were probably extolled in excess of its true worth. While it makes for good public relations, it says little about the day-to-day functioning of those whom it praises. Considering the time period in which it was necessary to staff such a large scale operation, it is in many respects remarkable that it was possible to assemble a staff at all, and while New York City probably contains the largest single reservoir of available talent for such a summer project in the United States, selection, training, assignment, and supervision of such a staff on short notice are difficult.

Staff Organization

During the month of May when the contract for the project was being negotiated, the staff consisted of the Coordinator of the project (on loan from the National Urban League), his secretary, and three other staff persons (on loan from HARYOU).

Recruitment for the remaining staff commenced in June. The administrative staff (central administration) for the project, as set forth in the proposal requesting funds, envisioned the following key professional personnel: project coordinator, assistant program coordinator, assistant to project director, business manager, personnel director, purchasing agent, bookkeeper, evaluation director, assistant evaluation director, and remedial reading director.

In addition, of course, each of the four major prime contractors—Associated Community Teams (ACT), Harlem Administrative Committee (HAC), Harlem Neighborhood Association (HANA), and the Urban League of Greater New York—was expected to include such professional supervisory personnel as necessary to perform adequately its obligations under the terms of the contract. Each prime contract agency agreed to assign certain of its professional personnel as supervisors for the duration of the project. If such personnel did not exist within the agency, it was expected that these people would be hired. Likewise, it was expected that each of the ninety-eight neighborhood organizations would either assign from its staff or hire the necessary supervisory personnel to train, teach, or supervise the youth assigned to the agency.

The major responsibility for the administration of the summer project, however, rested with the central administrative offices. As the project developed, certain administrative positions were added and others deleted in accordance with the needs of the project. By the time the project had reached mid-point, the major professional personnel charged with the administration of the project were the following: project coordinator, executive assistant to the coordinator, associate coordinator (in charge of Program Development and Training), director of remedial reading, medical officer, director of community relations and public relations, director of job development and guidance, evaluation directors (3), comptroller, assistant comptroller, legal assistant, business manager, and supply expediter.

A comparison of the list of projected professional personnel formulated during the planning stages of the project and the actual completed roster of administrative positions reveals the changes which were necessitated by the demands of the project as it unfolded. Several new posts which had not been envisioned were added. Inasmuch as hundreds of contracts were required and various other legal problems developed, it was necessary to add a legal office. This office was established July 19, and ultimately included a staff of eleven persons.

The initial proposal envisioned a business manager, a purchasing agent, and a bookkeeper. During the course of the project, however, it was necessary to increase greatly this staff. It ultimately included both a comptroller and an assistant comptroller. The office then assumed responsibility for purchasing and renting of supplies and equipment, and preparing and issuing salary checks for the youth and the adult staff of the project.

The evaluation staff, which ultimately was given autonomy from the project staff but which continued to function as a quasi-administrative office, was reorganized so that responsibility for the evaluation of the project was shared by three persons serving as co-directors. The position of assistant director of evaluation was deleted.

As the project developed, it was decided to add the post of director of job development and guidance. This office was organized August 5, the sixth week of the project, to deal with such problems as encouraging those youth still in school to return, placing those youth eligible for work in suitable jobs, and assisting those eligible for college by ascertaining scholarships available and other forms of financial assistance.

The problem of relations with the Harlem community, and public relations in general, was not envisioned early in the planning phases of the project. The demands of the program required an office of Community Relations and Public Relations. Ultimately this office was responsible for a variety of functions encompassing six major activities.

Finally, it was necessary to include a staff medical unit rather than a contractual arrangement with an outside agency because of the necessity for providing continuing physical examinations for youth enrolled in the project.

In addition to the above changes in personnel requirements, several other minor revisions resulted from the needs of the project. The post of director of personnel was assigned to the assistant to the project coordinator. The functions of bookkeeper and purchasing agent were transferred to HARYOU's comptroller's office, the business manager, and the supply office. These changes led to a more efficient operation of the project, except for fiscal problems, although many arose after the project was well underway. Assisting these key personnel was a large battery of assistants, secretaries, and clerks.

Recruitment

The problems involved in recruiting staff to fill the positions outlined above were many. The recruitment was rendered more difficult because of the short time span within which it had to be accomplished. Furthermore, prospective candidates for positions must have been willing to work for a period of ten weeks, after which it would be necessary to secure further employment elsewhere. Since the project was scheduled for ten weeks of summer, it was possible to draw upon public schools and colleges for short-term employees.

Since this project was designed for Central Harlem, and since its major (although unstated) goal was the containment of violence in this area, it would have been desirable to staff the entire project with personnel indigenous to the community. However, circumstances precluded such a development. It was necessary to fill the key posts with the most qualified available personnel no matter where they lived. One of the serious staffing problems faced by social agencies and schools in the black community is that they must often leave the area to secure personnel who meet the formal requirements of education and training.

Another problem faced by such institutions and one encountered by Project Uplift is that frequently white applicants who are unable to secure adequate positions in "white" agencies and institutions seize upon the opportunity to align themselves with those concerned with serving blacks. Often these people are not prepared for the positions for which they apply, but in the rush to "integrate" the staff, whites are accepted for positions for which blacks with comparable training and experience are rejected. In the present case, the staff of the project was racially integrated, and the white staff members ultimately selected appeared to be the individuals best suited for the positions. They were a visible minority, and they worked well with black staff members. Based on the experience of this and similar projects, the depressed areas contain an impressive array of indigenous leaders who perform well when given the opportunity.

In general one might say that given the circumstances under which the recruiting took place, an adequate staff was assembled to administer the project. This did not occur without a series of problems. One of the most serious problems confronted by the summer project was occasioned by the circumstances under which it was forced to operate. An earlier decision had been made that the project would be sponsored by the existing anti-poverty agency in Central Harlem—HARYOU. Part of the agreement stipulated that this agency would be responsible for assembling the initial staff of professional personnel for the project. That is, they would lend the project its initial staff members except for the Project Coordinator who was made available by the National Urban League. One of the responsibilities left to HARYOU was that of the personnel department. The personnel director for the agency therefore assumed the responsibility for certifying any personnel recommended by the Project Coordinator or his assistants. The agency naturally had established procedures for such operations and although the assembling of the summer project staff was of necessity a "crash" operation, it operated with a rigidity which was not amenable to the task which was necessary in this case. Thus, anyone proposed for a position who had been interviewed and approved by the Project Coordinator would then be sent to the personnel officer for the agency who processed the application in the same manner as applications for a permanent position with the agency. Thus, several staff appointees were required to work for weeks without knowing whether or not they would ultimately be approved and thereby paid for their services. The processing of an application for a professional position can require as much time as several weeks, even in small operations, and in an agency where funds were derived from federal, state and municipal sources, the formalities required are intensified. It is frequently necessary in such circumstances as those surrounding Project Uplift to forego some of the customary formalities if the project is to get under-way in the short time allocated.

The Project's "Cabinet" Officers

To a great extent whether the project operated at all depended upon the key professional personnel ultimately responsible for the various aspects of its operation. These people became known as "cabinet officers." They were the sixteen key personnel for the summer project. Whether or not their functions were adequately performed depended upon the assistance they received from the remaining 395 staff members in the central administrative office as well as the thousands of youth enrolled and the hundreds of supervisors in the four prime contract agencies and the 98 neighborhood organizations. However, since these sixteen individuals were ultimately responsible for the operation of the various administrative arms of the project, primary discussion will focus on them.

The Project Coordinator, responsible for the over-all operation of the project, was made available to the project by the National Urban League. He was a young official, who had specialized in education for the Urban League. While knowledgeable about the entire project, he concerned himself with the selection of key professional personnel. He, therefore, assumed that once a task had been delegated to a cabinet officer, it would be adequately performed. This was in part necessitated by the size and nature of the project. The Coordinator was required to spend a significant proportion of his time negotiating with federal, state, and city officials for additional funds and other requirements for the project. It was therefore impossible for him to "police" the entire operation of the project. The assumption by the Coordinator that once given, instructions would be implemented, posed serious problems during the course of the summer. For example, when it was decided that a legal assistant was necessary, the Coordinator announced that a young man who had been assigned to the personnel office would assume this function. This was an important post and required a well-trained lawyer. The personnel assistant represented himself as a recent graduate from the law school of a prestigious university. It was ultimately learned, however, not only that he was not a licensed lawyer, but that he had never attended law school. Therefore, it was necessary to find a lawyer who could process the many contracts between the administrative offices and the many subcontractors, and perform other legal functions.

In another case, also involving a member in the personnel department, an employee, during the middle of summer, announced that the Ph.D. degree had just been awarded to her. Further checking disclosed, however, that the degree to which she referred was not an earned doctorate from a reputable university, but rather one which had been acquired from a Canadian mail-order college after the payment of a certain amount of money. Because of the lack of training and experience, this employee had been partially responsible for the massive confusion in the personnel office at the beginning of summer.

Although the Coordinator was not a resident of Harlem he put forth every effort to understand the community. He frequently conveyed the impression that he had been convinced that a ten-week summer project could succeed in curing many of the social ills of the community. Such was the enthusiasm with which he approached the project. As a salesman for the project he was instrumental in generating a spirit of dedication among other administrators. It was difficult to say "no" to his requests. Nor was his salesmanship limited to employees of the project. He frequently met with businessmen in the city and persuaded them to devote money, materials, and services to the project.

As an administrator, the Coordinator operated with a degree of flexibility which served well the ends of the project. Although bound by a government contract to allocate funds to the activities designated therein, he was willing to encompass other activities in the Harlem community which he considered worthy of funds. Several on-going activities in Harlem applied to make their programs part of the summer project. The Coordinator studied these activities and where possible, funds and staff were made available to support seemingly worthy endeavors. Such activities may not have been eligible had a strict interpretation of the terms of the contract been applied, but on occasion the contract was interpreted broadly enough to encompass programs which may not have been able to operate otherwise. For example, a theater group was funded through the day camp budget. In general, the approach appeared to be that if an activity could further the general aims of the project, that is, if it could serve to contain the tensions in the area, the contract should be interpreted broadly enough to encompass it. Needless to say, such actions were frequently unpopular, especially with the parent agency.

It should probably be added that the Project Coordinator was forced to resign from the project before its completion. His resignation was a highly publicized event. Although the project had been scheduled to be terminated at the beginning of the school year, severe pressures for jobs for non-school age employees forced several extensions of the project until well into November. By this time there had been two acting coordinators who succeeded the original one. The circumstances surrounding the dismissal of the Coordinator are vague, but there was growing friction between him and the director of the parent agency, HARYOU. In the middle of September he was dismissed by the Board of Directors of HARYOU. Charges were made against him by the Board, and he made countercharges against the director of the parent agency. The ostensible reason for his dismissal was that he had confiscated office records and had them stored at home. In any case, it was a fairly widely shared opinion by the members of his staff that the Coordinator performed the task of chief administrative officer for the project with a high degree of efficiency.

The executive assistant to the Coordinator had been an employee of the parent agency before coming to the summer project. In her position as executive assistant she functioned as personnel officer. A person of many acknowledged talents, she was improperly utilized in the position of personnel officer, as evidenced by the confusion in the personnel office. Her qualifications for the post stemmed from past experience as opposed to formal training. In an operation of such magnitude, it is necessary for the personnel procedures to be routinely standardized, and exceptional cases may be more efficiently handled by a specially designated person. Yet the executive assistant assumed full responsibility for handling all cases and all problems no matter how minor. This made for improved morale among employees faced with problems, but it hardly contributed to the efficient operation of the personnel office. It was not at all uncommon to see a line of employees in front of the executive assistant's office when a matter of policy was awaiting a decision or a basket of letters and memoranda needed signatures.

Because of her personal magnetism and her willingness to consult with any employee at almost any time, the executive assistant performed a worthwhile morale function which should not be minimized. She spent hours listening to the multitude of problems which the supporting staff brought with them. Whenever she encountered an enrollee with an "anti-social" record she endeavored to place him in a responsible position as a means of instilling a sense of self-worth in him. In many cases she was able through this technique to "rehabilitate" individuals who had been habitual law violators. For example, when a young unwed mother who had earned a living as a prostitute came to her attention, she employed her in her office, and by the end of summer she had rented an apartment and taken a greater interest in her child. Furthermore, the executive assistant is reported to have obtained several scholarships at residential colleges for drug addicts who were on the road to recovery.

Although the executive assistant performed a worthwhile service to the project, her talents as director of personnel were improperly utilized. Recognizing this, she concentrated on activities for which she was especially well suited. Thereby she neglected many of the responsibilities which she was expected to perform. Toward the end of the summer, the executive assistant was reassigned to duties more commensurate with her skills.

The associate coordinator's main function in the project was program development and training. This was one of the major administrative functions in the project, and was assumed by a professor from a local college. She came to the project with vast experience in both teaching and administration in social welfare agencies. The training aspect of the associate coordinator's office lagged noticeably behind the program development aspect. In this case, the difficulties encountered were rightfully those resulting from the personnel office's initial ineptness rather than from the faulty operation of this office. For example, it had been planned that all youth enrolled in the project would be trained at central administration before entering the neighborhood organizations for assignment to work tasks. Because of difficulties in processing applications few (less than 200) of the youth received training at central administration. It then became necessary to provide assistance to neighborhood organizations in an effort to train enrollees.

The associate coordinator's main function after all programs were underway was consultation with the various agencies in order to insure that they were operating in compliance with the terms of the contract. In addition, where weaknesses appeared in an agency, the associate coordinator attempted to strengthen programs. This was an especially difficult task because many of the smaller organizations interpreted her function as that of spying. Cast in such a role, it was inevitable that difficulties would develop with the directors of these agencies.

Because of long experience with social service agencies and especially those serving youth, the associate coordinator was well trained for the position she occupied. Nevertheless, during the summer strained personal relations developed between the associate coordinator and virtually all other staff members, including the Project Coordinator. This situation adversely affected the smooth operation of several aspects of the project. By the end of summer the associate coordinator had antagonized the officials in the project and the contract agencies.

If they were asked to nominate the program in the project which was most successful, the likelihood is that a majority of the administrative officials would name the remedial reading program. The success of this massive operation can be directly attributed to its director who had resigned from college teaching and had agreed to direct this program although she had little experience with remedial education. Her major gifts, in addition to her manifest intelligence, were dedication, patience, imagination, and a love of children. In her quiet way, when she recognized that many aspects of the remedial reading program were impractical in the time allocated, she embarked upon a revision of the program which served some 1,150 Central Harlem youth in remedial reading and mathematics. The ingenuity of the director of this program was evidenced by the way in which she obtained space to teach these young people. When more space was needed she canvassed the Harlem area and located classrooms in unused schools, churches, and community centers in public housing projects.

All of the enrollees in the remedial reading program were expected to work as remedial reading teachers for the youth to be served by this activity. However, it was discovered that some of the younger enrollees could not read well enough to be teachers. She then revised her program to include a work-study program for these young people. As part of this program they were required to read books and write compositions. Other activities for them included trips to museums and libraries. In this way those who could not be utilized as teachers participated in an intellectual development program.

As with the other administrators in the summer project, the director of remedial reading in some respects fell short of the goal expected of this program. For example, the contract for the project stipulated that special teaching techniques be utilized which were so designed that "virtually any literate adult . . . can be an effective instructor for a group of ten people." With this plan it was hypothesized that "as little as twenty hours of instruction can produce an average reading gain of one year." The suggested method was not utilized, and although the director of this activity conducted the program with imagination, it was not possible to test the second hypothesis. This aspect of the program was crucial because a vast majority of youth in Central Harlem read below their grade level.

The medical officer apparently succeeded in giving a cursory physical examination to the more than 4,000 enrollees. In performing this task he was assisted by twenty-five nurses and nurses' aides and thirty doctors from an organization known as the Interfaith Health Movement. The examinations were accomplished in the early stages of the project, and after the first few weeks it was impossible to contact him for an interview. Repeated attempts over a period of two months failed to secure an appointment. There was no medical officer for the project after the initial physical examinations were accomplished.

Among the more difficult tasks in the project were those of community relations and public relations. These combined offices were headed by a young woman, a former official in the Congress of Racial Equality. Her previous experience had been in community organization, which apparently made her well suited for the post. Assisted by a large staff of young workers, the director diligently performed the difficult tasks of relations with the larger Harlem community and public relations in general. Among other things, they published an eight-page weekly newspaper, organized an art department, sponsored an art gallery, founded a dance company, and made a rather haphazard survey of the community.

There is some evidence that the activities undertaken by the community relations-public relations office were beyond the scope of the capabilities of that office and of its director. For example, the initial proposal for the project stipulated that a survey of the community be undertaken. This is a highly specialized activity which requires special skills if performed properly. Yet the director of this office assumed responsibility for this activity even after the evaluation section declined because of time. The result of their efforts was a badly written report which was of no value whatsoever.

It is quite likely that the dual functions of this office should have been separated. Some activities were performed well, others badly. The office performed with great skill such tasks as the publication of the newspaper, the formation of the dance group, and the parade and festival which signaled the end of the project. Their relations with the comparable office in the parent agency were somewhat less than harmonious.

The office of job development and guidance was conceived and organized toward the end of the summer. The director of this office had been transferred from the office of personnel. Prior to joining the staff of the project she had worked as a free-lance writer for magazines. Insofar as is known, nothing in her experience had especially equipped her for this position or for the personnel office, although she had been a student of personnel at a local university. Nevertheless, several of the objectives set for this office materialized. It was reported that nearly 1,000 part-time jobs were secured for the youth, and that many of them were encouraged to return to high school or to college. Furthermore, some eighty college scholarships were obtained for enrollees.

Clearly the office of job development and guidance was at a disadvantage because it was established toward the end of summer. Furthermore, adequate office space was not provided until

September 1, slightly more than one week before the end of the project. However, while it was in operation its director never clearly coordinated the various activities of this office. Often there was confusion. For example, one of the objectives was the establishment of a scholarship fund to help prospective college students in need of financial assistance. Such a fund was never established, and toward the beginning of the school year, prospective students were literally given the run-around about scholarship aid available at local colleges.

It must be added, however, that many of the problems encountered by this office were not caused by its director. They stemmed mainly from the delay in establishing the office and from personnel and space shortages.

The task of evaluating the project during its operation and after its completion was the responsibility of the evaluation office. Initially it had been proposed that the evaluators be a regular part of the project staff. However, it was later decided that in order to produce as objective an evaluation as possible the responsibility should be subcontracted to an independent agency. Ultimately the responsibility for evaluating the project was shared by three social scientists. Two of them were teachers at a local college, and the third was a research administrator for a commercial research organization. They were assisted by a staff of some fifteen assistants, statistical clerks, and secretaries. As a means of evaluating the project more than five thousand interviews, observations, and questionnaires were conducted or administered by the evaluation office during the duration of the project.

It was generally agreed that the evaluation office was competently staffed for the difficult task of evaluating the project. Each of its directors had come to the project with both training and experience in the area of social research. The directors apportioned the work among themselves and in general they worked well together. Furthermore, they were assisted by a competent staff of assistants. Difficulties arose from time to time because of the rather ambiguous status of the office. The directors were physically based with other members of the central administration, and many of the employees of this office were on the payroll of the central administration. Yet, they retained a degree of autonomy. A separate contract for the evaluation had been negotiated directly with the Office of Economic Opportunity, and the final evaluation report was the property of this agency. Such a situation made for difficulties with central administration, the contract agencies, neighborhood organizations, and the parent organization which maintained its own research office.

Perhaps two of the most difficult problems facing the directors of this office were the lack of availability of enrollees and supervisors throughout the project for interviewing. In this connection most of the administrative officials, especially the Project Coordinator, were cooperative, but no more than half of the enrollees could be located for the survey at either the beginning or the end of the project. Furthermore, the directors were unable to interview several key administrative personnel because they simply would not make themselves available.

The office of the comptroller and that of his assistant were among the most controversial in the project. The comptroller was an employee of the parent organization, while his assistant was appointed for the summer project only. The comptroller had been a finance officer in the army and his assistant had worked as a certified public accountant. Because of the inflexibility of the office and its continuing relations with the parent organization, it was difficult to get funds for supplies and equipment, and the payroll was invariably either late or inaccurate. Part of the payroll difficulties stemmed from what is apparently an unorthodox, but in this case understandable, procedure. Funds for the project were finally made available after it was already underway. Since a vast majority of employees were in severe need of funds, it was necessary to pay them for their services rendered before the federal funds had been received. Therefore, funds from the parent agency were transferred to the account of the summer project. This "commingling" of funds posed problems which had not been solved by the parent agency a year after the termination of the project. It should be added here that midway through the summer project the comptroller was discharged from his duties at which time his assistant assumed major responsibility. The constant delay in payment to the youth enrolled in the project made for serious problems of morale throughout the summer. Part of the difficulties stemmed, first, from the fact that the comptroller did not request sufficient material; second, from the volume of work involved in record keeping for an additional 5,000 people without sufficient increase in personnel; and, third, from the adoption of new procedures to meet the new demands.

Like many other arms of the administration of the project, the legal office was organized after the project was well underway. It was ultimately headed by a lawyer who was assisted by a staff of eleven assistants. Its director came to the project with extensive experience in legal assistance to Harlem's poor. Under his supervision this office dealt with the many legal problems facing the project ranging anywhere from the preparation and execution of nearly 200 contracts to cases of attempted rape.

The position of business manager was retained through the summer although this office as a separate administrative agency never really existed. The functions initially set for this office were transferred to the supply office and others in the comptroller's office such as the purchasing agent and the bookkeeper. Major responsibility was assumed by the bookkeeper, who, although arriving late, managed to institute procedures which led to more efficient payroll practices during the later stages of the project.

Finally, the supply office, like many of the other administrative agencies, came into being after the project was underway. This was necessitated by the need to purchase, rent, and distribute a vast amount of equipment such as typewriters, desks, chairs, air conditioners, etc. The person in charge of this office had come to the project from the parent agency, and because the program was already underway when the office was established, his job was a difficult one. In addition to supplying the central administrative offices, he was responsible for providing supplies to each of the four prime contract agencies and the ninety-eight neighborhood organizations. Few departments in the project faced as many problems as did the supply office. However, assisted by a staff of nearly one hundred (93), the supply officer managed to perform a staggering number of tasks. In addition, it is worth noting that, in spite of constant difficulties and long working hours, he managed to retain a calmness under such conditions of stress. Furthermore, he was always willing to circumvent the formal chain of command in order to provide the supplies essential to the operation of the program when necessary.

In spite of the many virtues of the supply officer, his operation posed problems for several of the other administrators as well as the contract agencies and neighborhood organizations. Frequently it was necessary to wait so long for supplies that when they arrived they were of no value. One of the most persistent complaints of supervisors in the field was that their work was delayed because of lack of supplies. It should be noted that these difficulties were frequently caused by the comptroller's office which ultimately controlled all funds for supplies and equipment.

The supply office was in a constant state of turmoil. Perhaps because their duties were so diverse it was impossible to perform many of them efficiently. For example, while the supply office may have been executing orders from elsewhere, they were nevertheless responsible for moving most offices in the project two or three times in the short period of ten weeks. This made for changes in locks on doors and it was not at all uncommon for staffs to be locked out of their offices. Rental companies frequently picked up typewriters without warning, and electric typewriters were more often inoperable than not.

The Staff of the Contract Agencies

Considerably less is known about the personnel directly responsible to the summer project but who were employed for that purpose by the four prime contract agencies and the ninety-eight neighborhood organizations. It seems clear, however, that inasmuch as the four prime contract agencies were selected to participate in the project because of their reputations as professionally operated social service agencies in Central Harlem, they no doubt operated in a more professional manner than the neighborhood organizations. The neighborhood organizations may be categorized by four different types of activity: block association, church, community center, and tenants group.

Of the ninety-eight neighborhood organizations, a majority were churches. For example, one of the major activities in the summer project was a network of day camp center programs. Sixty-eight of these centers were established throughout Central Harlem by one of the four prime contract agencies—Associated Community Teams—and of that number about half were operated by churches. These churches varied widely in their operation. For example, the Abyssinian Baptist Church, the Protestant church with the largest membership in the United States and a long-standing leader in social services in Harlem with an impressive professional staff, operated a day camp. At the other extreme, there were many churches which participated and which were situated in store-fronts with few members, and part-time ministers as the chief officials. In some cases the smaller churches employed special supervisory personnel for activities operated for the summer project and others depended upon the assistance of the central administration to supply enrollees for this purpose.

Block associations and tenants groups tend to be loosely organized, often depending on volunteers for staff. However, many of these organizations operate with a degree of efficiency which exceeds that of agencies staffed with professionals. On the whole, community centers are staffed by professional social workers who are trained in group work with youth. While some of these neighborhood organizations contributed little to the summer project, reports indicate that they were in general staffed with competent personnel who provided Harlem youth with such services as arts, crafts, music, dancing, drama, remedial education, sewing, field trips, and films. Depending upon the program, lunch was provided and parents often served as volunteers.

Each of the four major contract agencies maintained large staffs of social workers and other professional personnel who served as supervisors for the enrollees assigned to their agencies by the summer project. The largest of these agencies was Associated Community Teams, which is an affiliate of HARYOU but which is administratively autonomous. The responsibilities of this agency to the summer project included the operation of day and resident camps, and athletic workshops. The personnel directly responsible to the summer project included thirty-two professional staff members, twenty-five office personnel, and

140 supervisors. This staff worked directly with the 17,000 youth served by the agency during the summer.

The Urban League of Greater New York was responsible for two aspects of the summer project—tree planting and building repairs. These activities were supervised by a staff of thirty-three, each of whom was a specialist in the activity. The tree planting program lagged behind building repairs because of difficulties in securing permission to plant trees on city streets during the summer months. All reports indicate, however, that the supervisory staff in both of these activities performed their tasks as efficiently as circumstances permitted.

The Harlem Administrative Committee was responsible for three of the activities in the summer project—emergency home-maker service, historical landmarks, and information booths. A social worker, assisted by six supervisors, was responsible for this program. For a variety of reasons, the emergency homemaker service designed to assist needy families in Harlem, and the historical landmarks program designed to identify sites of historical events and the birthplaces of Harlemites who had made significant contributions to American life, never really developed. The information booths program was delayed in its operation. Nevertheless, this small staff of supervisors was able to establish five information booths to assist the residents of Central Harlem with information about New York City and available social services. It should be added that the five booths were rarely manned, and were more often closed than open.

Harlem Neighborhood Association was responsible for the vest-pocket park program. The agency is staffed by a group of social workers who utilized twenty-three supervisors in connection with their two summer project activities. The objective of this activity was to clear and construct vest-pocket parks on ten vacant lots in Central Harlem. By the end of the summer, this objective had not been fulfilled because of the necessity for negotiating leases for the property. The completed vest-pocket parks were highly praised, and there is every indication that the activity would have achieved its goal if time had not been lost in negotiating for leases.

While less is known about the administrators of the four prime contract agencies and those who worked directly with the enrollees in the field than about those in central administration, some appraisal of them can be made from a review of their activities and the extent to which they accomplished what they set out to do. With the several exceptions noted above, these people generally worked diligently to fulfill the tasks to which they were assigned.

More than 200 supervisors were responsible for the activities to which the youth were assigned. In many cases these supervisors worked directly with the community, but in general they served as intermediaries between the youth enrolled in the project and community population to be served.

Soon after the program was underway, a survey was made of supervisors by the evaluation staff. About half of them worked in the day camps program, with building repairs and tree planting occupying about one-fourth of the total. The remaining one-fourth were assigned to such other activities as vest-pocket parks, historical landmarks, neighborhood development, information booths, and the other activities of the summer project.

The supervisors, most of whom were indigenous to the Harlem community, had, in general, attained a high degree of formal education. Eighty per cent had completed some college training, with more than one-fourth (28 per cent) having graduated from college, and about one-third (32 per cent) having attended graduate or professional schools. Two-thirds (66 per cent) held some form of earned degree, one-fifth of them Masters' degrees.

The supervisors employed in the project represented a variety of fields of study. About one-fourth (24 per cent) were in education, and 15 per cent had been working in social sciences. Other fields represented were music and dance (8 per cent), fine arts (6 per cent), physical education (6 per cent), physical sciences (6 per cent), religion (6 per cent), and business (5 per cent).

The supervisors joined the summer project with a high degree of motivation. A vast majority (65 per cent) gave as the reason for joining that they wanted to be of assistance to the youth of Harlem. That is, their motivation was an altruistic one. Of the other reasons given, few of them were economic. The enrollees who were directly responsible to the supervisors throughout the summer, praised the supervisors at the end of the summer. Most (83 per cent) reported that their supervisors had at least done a "good job." Of those who did not praise them, most rated their performance as "fair" with few (4 per cent) rating their performance as "poor."

Supervisors were again questioned at the end of the project. In general, they reported that the program to which they had been assigned had been successful. A majority (55 per cent) rated it "very successful" while a minority rated it "somewhat successful."

In general, then, the picture of the supervisors in the summer project is one of an intelligent, well-trained, and dedicated group eager to assist in improving the conditions of Harlem. Their primary concern was with the youth whom they supervised, and the enrollees appeared to feel that, as supervisors, they had performed their functions well.

Staff Relations

Each of the administrative units in Project Uplift discharged its responsibilities more or less adequately. Some of them, mainly because of the persons in charge, managed to achieve outstanding success in their operations. But in order for the program as a whole to accomplish its stated and unstated goals, cooperation between the various offices was essential. Because of the nature of the project several sets of administrative interrelationships were necessitated. In the first place, there were the relationships between the various personnel in central administration. In addition, since the project was funded through HAR-YOU, there were relationships between the staff of the project and the permanent employees of that organization. Finally, cooperation between the administrative officers and the contract agencies and neighborhood organizations occasioned still another set of relationships. Needless to say, such complexity is likely to pose problems.

The Project Coordinator was frequently placed in a difficult position because of relations between the project and the parent organization, and because of the need to spend time in consultations with federal, state, and city officials. These considerations meant that much of the time which should have been devoted to the administration of the project was spent otherwise. He, therefore, relied on staff appointments which in some cases proved to be an unwise procedure. For example, at the inception of the project, if the Coordinator had devoted more time to the project it is likely that much of the confused personnel situation could have been avoided. In addition, the frequent absence of the Coordinator led to some friction between staff members. Frequently, their roles had not been well defined or additional responsibilities had been assigned as when one department was given the additional responsibility of "policing" programs in the day camp centers. The director of the unit interpreted this responsibility as including the approving of supply requests coming from these centers. This led to friction with the supply officer who had previously held this responsibility. In general, however, personnel in the various departments worked well together, and with the exception of the associate coordinator they maintained amicable relationships.

While HARYOU was the logical choice as applicant agency for the summer project, it was unprepared for the task. The administrative responsibilities created by the addition of 4,500 youth and the more than 400 administrative personnel posed problems from which the agency has yet to recover. Before enumerating areas of conflict between members of the summer project staff and those of the permanent staff of the agency, it should be noted that the agency did provide several of the initial professional personnel in an effort to get the project underway, and that on the whole relations between these two staffs were more friendly and cooperative than hostile. However, there were some areas of conflict. Some members of the permanent staff resented the influx of temporary summer employees. This made for problems of space and created serious problems around the use of the single elevator which may have been adequate for a small staff but which was inadequate now that the building was crowded.

Members of the staff of HARYOU were concerned that the summer project be clearly identified as part of the larger parent organization. Inasmuch as the summer project maintained its own public relations staff this office frequently came into conflict with the permanent public relations office. Items released by the project public relations office frequently neglected to mention the parent agency, and press releases about the summer project from the agency public relations office frequently neglected to mention Project Uplift. As a result, it sometimes appeared that the Coordinator and the director of the parent agency were involved in a duel for publicity.

One of the most serious areas of conflict between the two groups was no doubt that stemming from the office of the comptroller. Relations were ultimately such that it was impossible for the Coordinator to exert much influence over either the acquisition of supplies or difficulties stemming from delayed and inaccurate payrolls.

To a degree relations between individuals in the summer program and the parent agency were paralleled by those between the summer program staff and the personnel of the various contracting agencies and the neighborhood organizations. Each of the prime contract agencies and neighborhood organizations was concerned with its "image." These organizations had on-going programs of their own, but since Project Uplift was such a massive operation it was difficult for them not to be overshadowed. In addition the central administration of the project had a special staff in the field for the purpose of assisting these agencies. This was frequently misinterpreted as spying. In any one day a small church which served as a day camp center could be visited by officials from the supply office, the Coordinator's office, program development and training, and the evaluation office. Consequently relations were often strained. There were occasional threats of law suits, and before the end of summer permanent antipathy had developed between some of these individuals.

Conclusions

The problems involved in staffing such a massive operation as Project Uplift in the short period of time allocated and on a short range basis are not difficult to understand. In many ways it is indeed remarkable that such a project as this achieved as many of its goals as it did. A vast majority of the staff members were hard working individuals who made contributions to the project to the extent of their capabilities. Part of the whole purpose of the project was the training which the 395 staff assistants received. It is characteristic of slum areas that few skilled personnel remain in the area. Harlem is devoid of places of employment for these people, and the area in general lacks the municipal services which other sections (of the city command. This is mainly because the area is inhabited by a powerless people. Why bother to provide more social services for these people, when it is unlikely that they pose much of a threat to the established leaders? Hence, the area is generally physically depressing. Consequently potential talent, where possible, chooses to leave the area for other parts of the city.

Added to this was the necessity to find skilled people for temporary employment. Most of the administrative assistants were residents of Central Harlem. That the project was able to recruit so many of them who were willing to work on a temporary basis indicates that in slum areas many talented people who are both willing to work and competent are unable to find work outside the area. Frequently during the summer project unusual talent was uncovered. These people could have performed a variety of tasks diligently and efficiently in private industry had they been given a chance. So frequently had they been rebuffed that they had simply discontinued their efforts to secure employment. A few examples serve to illustrate the point.

One stenographer with the project who had been unemployed for several years inquired about work after the summer project. Several corporations had expressed interest in hiring staff personnel when the project terminated. One of the major airlines requested a secretary. This young lady was referred to the personnel section of the company only to be offered a job as a filing clerk at seventy-five dollars weekly. They were surprised when a secretary with a Bachelor's degree refused the offer. White secretaries with her level of competence frequently earn twice the salary which was offered to her.

A young housewife who had spent several years as a statistical clerk in Washington, D.C., accepted a temporary position with the summer project. She had remained at home for the previous two years. Upon completion of the project she interviewed for several jobs but was unable to find one which was commensurate with her training and experience.

Finally, a young mother of seven children learned of the project after it had been underway for several weeks. She applied for the position of clerk typist and was hired. Since she lived in the area, it was possible for her to work to supplement her husband's inadequate income. Long after the project had been terminated she was searching for employment in the community so that she would not have to travel long distances from her children.

In each of the cases cited above, representing only a few of those which turned up during the summer project, the individuals performed at a high level of competence. They were eager to work, but they had been rebuffed so frequently that hope for finding suitable employment virtually died. The summer project was instrumental in uncovering many capable individuals who had simply not been permitted to engage in gainful employment. It is well known that many of the lesser administrative officials in the United States are people who have few special skills and who simply follow instructions. In this regard a vast majority of the individuals who worked in the summer project were indeed at least comparable to their counterparts in private industry and government. And, equally important, these individuals worked with a laudable degree of diligence.

CHAPTER FIVE

People in the Project: Youth

As already pointed out, Project Uplift ultimately developed into a vehicle designed to maintain "peace" in Harlem during the summer of 1965. Harlem had been the scene of "riots" the preceding summer, and the newspapers and self-styled spokesmen in the community continually warned of the "long, hot summer" ahead. The object, then, was to provide a means of offering some type of employment in order to keep the teenagers off the streets during the hot summer months. Although the project was originally conceived in March as a plan for beautifying Harlem slums, funds for such a program had not been made available. With the impending end of the school year, politicians in Washington and New York became increasingly interested in making certain that Harlem remain "cool" during the summer. Consequently on June 11, slightly more than two weeks before the end of the school year, it was announced that Harlem would be provided with the federal funds necessary to put a massive self-help summer program into effect. The project was designed to provide employment for thousands of youth ranging in age from fourteen through twenty-five.

Harlem youth were the central focus of the project. Technically, because of the organization of the project, it was designed to provide the youth with useful work experience in an effort to increase their job skills, and to provide for the strengthening of the neighborhood organizations in which they would be directly employed. If such were accomplished, it was felt that many neighborhood organizations would have a greater impact on the area with its proliferation of social problems. It should be reemphasized, however, based on public utterances of politicians, many of whom were responsible for the final allocation of funds, that one of the major objectives of the project remained the containment of "violence" in Central Harlem.

Recruitment

Inasmuch as the final proposal for the project was approved in Washington on June 25, just three days prior to the end of school, the recruitment of youth to be enrolled in the project presented many problems. Ultimately some 4,500 youth were enrolled. They were recruited through the use of mobile recruitment centers set up in strategic locations throughout Central Harlem. Announcements were made in the press and on the radio, and notices were posted throughout the area. Enrollees were to be residents of the area and were to be registered on a first-come, first-served basis.

This method posed some problems because several of the participating agencies in the area recruited enrollees independently and chaos resulted. After each enrollee had completed the necessary enrollment forms, he was given a receipt and directed to report to a definite location at a specified time. Administrative confusion and alleged reproduction of receipts resulted in enrolling many youth who were technically ineligible, and increased the total number of youth enrolled in the project to a number in excess of the budget allocations for paying them. Furthermore, because of the lack of time and lack of administrative experience with processing large numbers of people, the entire personnel system collapsed. The result was that several different sets of confusing and conflicting instructions were issued to these youth, many of whom wandered around for days in utter confusion.

During the early stages of the project the records kept on the youth were inadequate. For example, at no time during the first month of the project did a complete listing of the enrollees exist, with what is usually considered to be basic information (e.g., name, age, sex, and address). This lack, of course, affected the functioning of the various other agencies in the administrative staff such as payroll and training. To add to the confused situation, the temperature remained in the high eighties and nineties, and air conditioning was virtually non-existent. It was not at all uncommon to see a mother accompanying a son or daughter attempting to make sense out of the confusion. Invariably, they were directed to a series of offices, which may have required several hours, with the likelihood that they were as confused when they left the last office as they were when they entered the first.

Such massive confusion produced unfortunate consequences for the project. Several weeks after its initiation, it was said by personnel officials to have been oversubscribed. However, it was discovered that at the point where 3,000 youth were to have been enrolled (and enrollment was scheduled to occur in phases), fewer than 2,000 had been registered. The personnel office maintained, however, that the full number had been registered. But it was impossible to locate the more than 1,000 lost youth. Federal appropriations being what they are, if the project had enrolled fewer youth than stipulated in the grant, the excess money would have to be returned. Such a situation clearly would have been intolerable in one of the most depressed areas in the United States. Whatever else the project may have failed to accomplish, it did bring much needed money into the Harlem community. Therefore, a major attempt was made to recruit additional youth for this phase of the project. In the end some 1,500 more youth than initially planned for were enrolled in the project.

Preparing for Work

After an enrollee had been properly registered for work in Project Uplift, which was frequently a difficult task as a result of administrative confusion, and before he was assigned to a specific activity, he was administered a physical examination in keeping with the requirements of the city and state laws. The examination was performed by a battery of doctors and nurses, most of whom donated their services. At this point it was necessary for the school-age youth to secure working papers, again in accordance with city and state laws. By arrangement with the New York City Board of Education, working papers were issued at the same time that enrollees were given physical examinations.

Because several of the contract agencies assumed responsibility for recruiting youth already in attendance in their activities, the processing of the enrollees for physical examinations and working papers did not proceed according to schedule. Frequently several agencies would send hundreds of youth for physical examinations without the knowledge of the central administrative office, and the medical staff was unable to process them. For example, the physical examinations were performed in a church building made available for that purpose. On one occasion the minister reported to central administration that 750 enrollees had appeared at once in search of physical examinations. Hundreds had to be turned away, a frustrating experience for them especially since they knew they could not be employed (and hence paid) until the physical examination had been accomplished.

After having been certified physically fit to work, enrollees were to receive further instructions in the mail. Because of the confusion in the placement office, it was not at all uncommon for an enrollee to receive as many as three or four letters, signed by different officials with conflicting instructions. In this case, the difficulty appeared to stem from the lack of relevant experience in record keeping and the processing of job applications in an office which was completely staffed by teen-agers. In the meantime, requests continued to mount in central administration for enrollees from the various agencies. Needless to say, they could not be filled until the administrative confusion was somehow eliminated.

When the enrollees who were finally selected had completed physical examinations, they were supposed to receive intensive orientation over a period of several days. At the orientation sessions they were to have been briefed about the objectives of the project and their specific tasks within it. Such an arrangement required that they report to central administration in groups, depending upon their work assignments. For reasons which remain unclear, of the 4,500 youth in the program, only some 180 actually attended the orientation program. This situation led to many other complications. For example, an important aspect of the program involved a detailed study of the enrollees to be conducted both at the beginning and at the end of the project. It had been planned that the study would be a regular part of the administrative processing, specifically to be accomplished during the orientation. Since so few of them had participated in the orientation it became necessary somehow to assemble them at different times in order to administer rather lengthy and somewhat complicated questionnaires to them. It should be added that the personnel responsible for orientation eventually decided to conduct this activity after enrollees had been assigned to an agency.

Most of the programs in Project Uplift were finally staffed and underway during the second week in July. The enrollees settled down to work and faced the problems which were yet to develop, most notably being paid on time. For a program in a depressed area the failure to pay participants at the designated time can provoke problems of enormous magnitude. Most of the youth in the project were completely without funds, and the major incentive for enrolling was the pay offered. It is no wonder, then, that delayed and inaccurate payrolls loomed as one of the major sources of irritation throughout the summer.

Any analysis of the administrative difficulties present in this project would be incomplete without special mention of one of the major sources of these problems. As proposed, Project Uplift was designed in such a way that smooth administrative functioning was possible. One of the major difficulties, however, stemmed from the lack of administrative experience with processing large numbers of people. Suddenly, at the last minute, some 4,500 people were expected to be recruited, examined, trained, and assigned to nearly 100 different agencies to work. These 4,500 people were thrust upon an agency which had been accustomed to handling only hundreds of people. The machinery for such a task was not available, and when the funds were somehow withheld until after it was expected to be in operation, smooth functioning was too much to expect.

Job Assignments

In spite of the widespread administrative confusion, Project Uplift managed ultimately to provide income for some 4,500

youth in Central Harlem. These young people were designated as
aides, assistants, and associates. Aides were those who were
either fourteen or fifteen years of age, worked thirty-two hours
weekly and received $32.50 in salary. Assistants ranged in age
from sixteen through twenty-one, worked forty hours weekly,
and received $40. Associates ranged in age from twenty-two
through twenty-five, worked forty hours weekly, and were paid
$80. The amount of the weekly salary was based on age rather
than any prior work experience, although different tasks were
assigned depending upon age.

These 4,500 youth were assigned a multitude of tasks, depending upon the requirements, and many of the tasks they
performed, while not outlined in the initial proposal, reflected
changes in the program occurring during the course of the
summer.

While a vast majority of the enrollees were assigned to the
various neighborhood programs through the area, several of them
were assigned to central administration where they worked in
the various offices such as personnel, program development and
guidance, public relations and community relations, and supply.
In each case, however, the central administrative office was
headed by an adult with previous training and experience in the
area. Generally, the enrollees performed such tasks as typing and
other routine office work. There were notable exceptions, however. For example, the personnel office included a section on
youth placement. This office was operated by youths recruited
for the project and employed twenty-seven enrollees who served
in such capacities as assistant to the director of personnel, secretaries, clerk-typists, and messengers. While it is true that in this
function the enrollees no doubt contributed to the administrative confusion, it must be added that their contribution in this
regard was minimal.

In addition to the enrollees assigned to the personnel office,
the public relations and community relations section utilized enrollees in many capacities. A newspaper was written, edited, and
set-up by enrollees. They served as photographers, reviewed
plays performed by other enrollees, and in general covered each
of the programs included in the project. In addition to the newspaper, these enrollees staffed an art department which prepared

visual materials for distribution; they organized a dance team; they ran an art gallery; and they were responsible for disseminating nearly one half million pieces of literature during the official ten weeks of the project.

The vast majority of the young people were assigned to the fifteen special programs contracted to the various neighborhood organizations in Central Harlem. In these organizations they worked at such tasks as remedial reading and remedial mathematics, neighborhood development, day and resident camps, athletic workshops, building repairs, tree planting, information booths, emergency homemaker service, and the Black Arts Repertory Theatre. In some cases, the work assigned to an enrollee was routine and simply required his performing some perfunctory task. However, in many cases skill and imagination were required, and the tasks were performed with diligence, often consuming more than the allocated number of hours. In general the more responsibility delegated to an enrollee, the greater the diligence he showed performing the task. In some cases where an enrollee was assigned to an office but the supervisor failed to provide meaningful employment, he tended to idle away the time until payday. In some few cases where enrollees were bored because of lack of challenging work, they simply made an appearance daily, disappeared and returned to collect the pay check. And, of course, there were those enrollees who, no matter what the work task, simply showed up long enough to be entered on the payroll.

Specific Work Tasks

Enrollees in the summer project who were not assigned to office work in central administration worked either in one of the activities under the jurisdiction of an administrator from central headquarters or in one of the numerous activities contracted to one of the four prime contract agencies. In the latter case, the specific tasks they performed were under the sponsorship of one of the ninety-eight neighborhood organizations. As a means of discussing the specific tasks these youth performed during the summer, their work will be broken down according to the agency contractually responsible for the program. These are central administration, Associated Community Teams, The

Urban League of Greater New York, Harlem Administrative Committee, and Harlem Neighborhood Associations. Finally, several of the youth were assigned to special programs which were added during the course of the summer. These will be presented last.

Central Administration Programs. Three of the many activities of the summer project were administered by central administration. They were remedial reading, community surveys, and neighborhood development. Of the three, remedial reading was the largest and involved considerably more enrollees than the other two. This program was designed to provide remedial reading for children in the area, and ultimately utilized the services of seventy-five enrollees. Within this program enrollees performed a variety of tasks such as correcting deficiencies in reading skills and abilities; giving the child auditory, visual, and verbal experience with vocabulary; fostering growth in basic comprehension abilities, word meaning, thought units, sentence sense, paragraphs, and total selections.

Initially the enrollees in the remedial reading program were trained for their responsibilities in an in-service training course. Once this course was completed, those enrollees who had demonstrated their abilities as potential teachers were assigned to classes of students. Others were enrolled in a work-study program. Because the materials for this program arrived late in the summer it became necessary for enrollees and supervisors to secure adequate materials from home and to write and duplicate textbooks for classes. All reports indicate that the enrollees assigned to the remedial reading program were effective in their assignments. The supervisors in this program were unanimous in praise of the enrollees, as was the director of the program. Furthermore, the enrollees in this program had one of the best attendance records in the project. To some degree this is a measure of the effectiveness of the program and of their dedication to it.

The community survey associates were part of the community relations-public relations department. Specifically, the associates were to have two major functions: to survey the impact of the program on the larger community, and to assist block associations and tenant organizations. Approximately 125 enrollees, at all levels, were assigned to community survey associates. During the course of the summer they performed the following activities: 1) Tenants were assisted in filing housing complaints with the appropriate city agency; 2) An information sheet on housing was prepared and distributed to residents in the area; 3) Conferences were held with the United Block Association; 4) An attempt was made to document exploitation of residents by merchants through comparison shopping; 5) Interviews were held with 1,140 residents to determine whether or not they were registered to vote, and to encourage those who were not registered to do so; 6) Library research on black heritage was accomplished and discussion groups on this subject were held.

Since none of the five supervisors assigned to this section had experience in working in communities, the value of the work accomplished by the enrollees is somewhat dubious. This is unfortunate because this was an area where important work could have been done, and there is no evidence that the enrollees in community survey associates were any less diligent or dedicated than were others. Rather, the supervision given them was such that it would have been impossible for them to have done a more satisfactory job.

The neighborhood development program, like the community survey associates, was part of the community relations-public relations department. According to the original proposal this office was to have assigned enrollees to block associations, to evaluate each neighborhood organization in the project, and to supply supervisors for local groups. There is no evidence whatever that this unit of the summer project in fact existed. Therefore it must be assumed that no enrollees were assigned to it.

Associated Community Teams. The Associated Community Teams was responsible for three of the major activities in the summer project: day camps, resident camps, and athletic workshops. The first of these, the day camp program, was the largest single activity in the summer project. This program had two general objectives: to provide educational and recreational activities for children in Central Harlem, and to enrich the lives of the enrollees in the program. Nearly half (48 per cent) of the 4,500 enrollees were assigned to the day camp program. The activities performed by these enrollees varied according to the day camp to which they were assigned, but all the day centers included the following as part of their program: storytelling, games, music, dancing, arts and crafts, black history, remedial reading, and field trips. A vast majority of the enrollees assigned to these centers report having enjoyed working with children, and the evidence indicates that their work was effective.

The resident camps had essentially the same objectives as the day camps; however, since these camps were out-of-town, their attendance was limited to children from families in the lowest income brackets. Five such camps were operated in Colorado, Pennsylvania, and Minnesota. Inasmuch as these camps maintained their own staffs of counselors, few enrollees were engaged in these activities.

The athletic workshops were to provide organized, supervised athletic activities for the youth in Central Harlem. In achieving this goal, it was hypothesized that the enrollees in the project would be taught recreational skills, especially supervision. Altogether some 211 enrollees at all levels participated in the athletic workshops. It is estimated that these enrollees served some 10,000 children during the ten-week period. They supervised forty-five basketball teams, several track and field meets, and thirty softball teams.

The Urban League of Greater New York. Beautifying Central Harlem was the Urban League of Greater New York's contribution to the summer project. This involved two activities: tree planting and building repairs. The building repairs program was designed not only to repair buildings but also to contribute to the skills of the enrollees. Altogether some 465 enrollees were assigned to this program. Enrollees were organized into work units, under the supervision of an adult specialist for the purpose of cleaning, painting, and making minor repairs of buildings in an effort to beautify the community. Although some of the enrollees complained about the "hard, physical labor" required of them and although supplies were frequently delayed, these enrollees improved buildings in Central Harlem ranging from churches to theaters. Everything considered, this was one of the most successful activities in the summer project.

The objective of the tree planting activity was to plant 1,500 trees on the streets of Central Harlem. The enrollees were expected to prepare sites for the trees and plant them under supervision. They gained experience in preparing sites but not in actually planting trees because several complications developed and one tree was planted during the life of the project. (See Chapter VII.)

Harlem Administrative Committee. This agency assumed responsibility for three of the summer project activities: emergency homemaker service, historical landmarks, and information booths. The first of these activities endeavored to train and employ young women to serve as emergency homemakers for families in crisis situations. Some forty-three enrollees participated in this program. Their activities included a variety of tasks such as general cleaning, preparing food, and child care. Most of the families assisted indicated that they appreciated the services provided by these young women.

The historical landmarks program was designed to identify sites of historical events and the birthplaces of persons in the area who had made significant contributions to American society. Historical markers were to be placed on these sites. The enrollees assigned to this program did not succeed in this objective but they conducted a few guided tours, mainly to museums in the vicinity of Harlem.

The information booth program had as its objective the establishment of information booths on the streets of Harlem for the purpose of informing citizens of the area of social services available to them. The enrollees in this program manned five such booths and produced a seventy-page social service directory containing information about health, housing, and religious, educational, and entertainment facilities.

Harlem Neighborhood Association. This agency was responsible for one of the activities in the summer project: vest-pocket parks. The objective of this program was to clear vacant lots in the area and construct vest-pocket parks on these sites. Altogether some 160 enrollees were assigned to this project. They worked at such tasks as clearing lots, reading and interpreting plans and specifications, and simple construction, under the guidance of supervisors. While they fell short of their goal of ten vest-pocket parks, by the end of summer they had constructed six such parks, and cleared space for the other four.

Special Programs. In addition to the foregoing basic programs, several new ones were developed during the course of the summer. One such program was the controversial Black Arts Repertory Theatre. Its aim was to involve enrollees in programs of drama, music, poetry, group discussions, and film making. This program attracted widespread attention, especially for its dramatic productions staged on the street corners and other outside locations throughout Harlem. Mainly because of the exceptional ability of its director, the activities of this program were well received. The exhibits, plays, recitals, and discussion groups were well attended and well received by audiences throughout the area, and in no activity did the enrollees work more diligently than in those sponsored by the Black Arts Repertory Theatre.

Another addition to the roster of summer project activities was the Harlem Olympics. This activity was held toward the end of summer. It utilized enrollees assigned to all phases of the project. Altogether twenty-four track and field events were sponsored, involving more than 300 athletes. This group had been selected from thousands of entrants who competed in earlier try-outs.

The summer project was terminated with a massive parade through Harlem and an all-afternoon festival in Central Park. Enrollees, under the guidance of supervisors, constructed thirty floats, and participated in seventeen bands and bugle corps for the parade. The parade terminated at the festival grounds. The festival consisted of a variety of exhibits and productions staged by groups of enrollees from the various activities in the summer project. There were art exhibits, poetry reading, dance troupes, dramatic productions, remedial reading demonstrations, and many other features. In general, the festival was well planned and executed, and involved a cross-section of enrollees from all of the activities which made up the massive summer project.

A Day in the Life of an Enrollee

The following represents a verbatim account, in his own words, of a typical work day for an enrollee in Project Uplift. This eighteen-year-old assistant, who has since graduated from college, worked with the Urban League of Greater New York's building repairs program.

"I was assigned to the 'beautification' program, which really meant painting, cleaning, and plastering old church buildings in the Harlem community. The pay for my 'services' was forty dollars per week. I was eighteen at the time and the group of boys that worked with me ranged from fourteen to eighteen years of age. These boys were from the immediate area of Harlem. The younger fellows in the fourteen age bracket were paid about twenty-seven dollars per week (take home pay). Our supervisor was a carpenter who had his own business in Harlem. This was an advantage for the boys who worked under him because he was able to show us how to construct things properly out of wood and to apply this in fixing structures in the old church buildings.

"The church officials were very receptive to our group when we came in to paint their buildings.

"Out of this background let us see how a typical day passed while in this program.

"8:15 A.M.—I reach the work site and sign in. My group is assigned to plaster and paint the interior of the Christian Reformed Church on 122nd Street. The boys gather around the steps of the church, and receive their specific instructions from the supervisor. Each fellow is given a specific task, such as sweeping the floor, plastering the walls, or painting the ceilings.

"8:30—Work begins on the church. I am instructed to take care of the tools and equipment. The tools include paint brushes, hammers, screw drivers, and trowels. I am held accountable for every tool at the work site. Therefore I keep a checklist of every person who takes a tool. After I clean out the paint brushes and dust the tools, I give out the specified tool to each worker. I then grab a paint brush myself and begin to work.

"9:00-12:00—I am engaged in painting the walls and ceilings of the basement of the church. Some other boys are plastering the walls so that they may prepare them for painting. Many times I have to 'get off' the ladder and go to the tool area to 'check in' and 'check out' tools.

"12:05-12:45—Lunch Break!!! We put the equipment in a convenient place and get something to eat.

"12:50—Work starts again. We are still in the basement area of the church. The rooms in the basement are large and dilapidated. Some of the boys are not plastering the walls correctly. The supervisor, consequently, brings the entire group together and goes over step by step the correct method of plastering. He also shows some of the boys how to fix the broken doors and chairs that are in the basement.

"1:00-3:30—We are still working on the basement level. The supervisor appoints two boys to go to the first floor to scrape the walls and ceilings, and generally prepare the first floor level for painting and cleaning.

"3:30-4:00—Clean up time!! Some of the boys sweep the dirt and debris from the floor and put it in the boxes. I clean the brushes, put the equipment back in order, get my street clothes on, and sign out."

Demographic Characteristics

Since Project Uplift was designed as an anti-poverty measure for Central Harlem, it might be expected that the youth enrolled in the project would be reasonably homogeneous insofar as background characteristics are concerned. They were about evenly divided between males and females, with a few more males than females. The younger enrollees tended to predominate, with about two-thirds of them being somewhere between fourteen and seventeen years of age.

With such an age span, it follows that a majority of the youth were enrolled in school at the time of the project. Altogether about one-fifth had graduated from high school, and a few of these were enrolled in colleges and universities. Harlem is reported to have a higher school drop-out rate than the City of New York as a whole, and an effort was made to determine the drop-out rate among enrollees in the project. Insofar as it could be determined, only 3 per cent of the enrollees were high school drop-outs. Such a low rate compared to what is generally reported for Central Harlem probably indicates that the measures used in the present study were inadequate. Also, this could indicate that the project did not succeed in reaching the youth it was designed to attract.

The families from which the enrollees came might be expected to represent among the most destitute families in New York City, that is, if they were truly representative of the families which the program was designed to assist. The average number of siblings per family was 3.4. The average weekly income was reported to have been $124.65, with more than one-third reporting total family incomes of less than $100 weekly. In many cases both parents were employed, and where such was the case the average earnings for the mother were less than fifty dollars weekly, while the average earnings for the father were about $100.

Low educational level of parents, in part, accounted for low incomes. About one-third of the enrollees reported that their fathers did not graduate from high school, and a similar proportion of mothers (30 per cent) left high school before graduation.

Generally, broken families are felt to be representative of the poor urban black youth. While such reports are frequently intended to indicate something about the "moral" standards of their parents, they describe the social conditions in which many of America's poor are forced to exist. Among the enrollees in Project Uplift, as nearly as could be determined, about one-half of the youth had lived in "broken homes" at some point during their schooling.

Finally, if one considers the youth not enrolled in school at the time of the project as eligible for the labor force, only about one-half of them were gainfully employed. Fully 48 per cent of the youth eligible for employment during this period were without work. In this regard, the project provided temporary employment during this period for hundreds of the youth of Central Harlem, and as an afterthought an agency was set up to attempt to secure jobs for those who would need them after the project had terminated.

Attitudes and Opinions

The attitudes of the black youth in America's urban slums have been the subject of much speculation. Politicians and other self-styled spokesmen persist in assaying the mood of these youth as though it was monolithic. Rarely are they asked their attitudes and opinions on issues; rather, middle-class blacks usually volunteer or are requested to serve as their spokesmen.

At the beginning of the project an attempt was made to survey the youth to find out what their attitudes and opinions were on a variety of issues. Again, at the end of the project these same youth were questioned in an attempt to determine if enrollment in the program and participation in a massive community action project had in any way affected these attitudes and opinions. One of the hypotheses underlying the entire project was that the experience in such a project would influence these youth positively, especially insofar as self-esteem and positive identification were concerned.

According to their own admission, the single greatest factor motivating the youth to enroll in the project was economic. A few of them listed such other factors as being of assistance to other youth in the area, but by and large their interest centered around the money they were paid for participating in the project. Such a finding is certainly not unexpected from youth in an area as depressed economically as is Harlem. Under such circumstances as these youth are forced to live, one could hardly expect altruism or some other noneconomic reason to have played a role in their action. Furthermore, the poorer the youth, the more inclined they were to list one of several economic factors as influencing their participation in the project.

At the beginning of the project the enrollees were also asked what they expected the project to accomplish. In spite of their desire (and need) to earn money during the summer, the enrollees entered the project with high expectations. In general, their expectations fell into three categories: 1) personal advancement, 2) assistance to other youth in the area, and 3) community improvement. On the whole, the enrollees expected to benefit from the project to a greater extent than they expected the community to benefit. That is, they appeared to realize that the problems in Central Harlem were of such magnitude that no ten-week program could begin to deal with them. Whether their personal improvement goal was achieved is open to question, especially since they expressed a hope that the program would improve their chances for the future.

*　　　*　　　*

One of the basic aims of the project as repeatedly stated at the outset and hypothesized in the proposal which served to request funds, was the improvement of the self-image of the enrollees. It is invariably assumed by most writers on the subject that to a significant degree having lived for centuries in a racist society has affected the self-esteem of black Americans. This low self-esteem is felt to be transmitted from one generation of blacks to the next in the same fashion as other aspects of the culture. In an effort to explore the self-concept of the enrollees, a personality test was utilized. This test was designed to compare their conception of themselves with their perception of the ideal personality. In general, the enrollees at the beginning of summer did not perceive of themselves as being significantly different from what they thought an ideal personality should be. On some items they thought of themselves as possessing more "adaptive" traits of personality than the ideal person, and on others less. The responses varied anywhere from high conceptions of self, as compared with the ideal, to relatively low conceptions of self.

The enrollees were given the same personality test at the end of the project to see if differences had resulted from enrollment in the project. It was found that no significant differences appeared in any one of the many categories used to measure conception of self. That is, the enrollees perceived of themselves in the same way at the end of the project as they had at the beginning. It should be re-emphasized that this conception of self was by no means a negative one. It is entirely possible that what the designers of the personality test perceived of as adaptive traits were not those so considered by the youth. For example, many of the enrollees perceived of the ideal person as one who is "shrewd and calculating" while few of them envisioned themselves in such terms. That is, life in the slums had taught them that some of what are considered "maladaptive" traits are actually functional for the individual in such circumstances. In similar fashion they perceive of the ideal personality as being considerably more "selfish" than they consider themselves.

In addition to a reasonably high conception of self, these youth readily acknowledged the need for improving their basic skills such as reading and writing, verbal expression and technical proficiency. Almost all of them recognized the importance of these skills for self-improvement if they were to make a satisfactory adjustment to a highly industrialized society. Furthermore, when asked what the most important thing about a job was for them, they invariably listed advancement.

The picture presented, then, is one of youth in the slums eager to advance themselves economically so that the poverty of their parents will not be transmitted to them.

*   *   *

How do the youth of Central Harlem feel about living there? Would they move out if they could? Do they prefer an all-black neighborhood? How do they feel about their neighbors? Answers to these questions were provided by the enrollees in the summer project. Their attitudes were decidedly mixed. The only question which showed any clear-cut feeling was the one on the racial character of the neighborhood they preferred, and attitudes toward their neighbors. A vast majority of them indicated a preference for racially mixed neighborhoods, and most of them responded favorably when asked to characterize their neighbors. Otherwise the responses were so varied that generalizations are hazardous. It should be added, however, that there was clearly no pattern of self-hate discernible from their responses.

The question of who among black leaders commands greatest admiration among the youth of the black community was raised with the enrollees in the summer project. The single most striking finding observed was that Martin Luther King, Jr., was selected by more of them than all the remaining names together, which included national personalities such as Ralph Bunche, Adam Clayton Powell, and Malcolm X, and such locally prominent personalities as Jesse Gray and LeRoi Jones. It came as somewhat of a surprise that Malcolm X was selected by only 5 per cent. There appeared to be no wholesale support of the more militant leaders over those who are usually regarded as moderates. Indeed, the more moderate leaders were selected more often than the militant ones. At the end of the project, however, when again presented with the same list, there was a definite tendency to select the more militant leaders over those who are considered to be more moderate. The exception again was Martin Luther King, Jr., who was clearly the most popular leader among the youth of the project. However, it appears that the experience of having been enrolled in Project Uplift had the effect of making for greater appreciation for militant black leadership.

Finally, the enrollees were asked to express their opinions about policemen. Charges of police brutality are widespread in Harlem, and the preceding summer "riots" were generated by the fatal shooting of a black teen-ager by a white policeman. One might suspect, then, that attitudes toward the police might be somewhat negative. When questioned, however, a vast majority of the respondents expressed positive or neutral attitudes toward the police. Only one respondent in ten expressed strongly negative views toward the police.

In addition to preference for leaders, the enrollees were also questioned again at the end of summer about attitudes toward the police and toward living in Harlem. In both of these areas there had been a substantial change in the ten-week period. Their attitudes about living in Harlem were more positive, and their attitudes about the police were more negative. While the general data on attitudes and opinions indicated that they had few fixed views in many of these areas, the likelihood is that after having been exposed to material on African and Afro-American history, they began to develop greater positive identification. That is, they developed greater feelings of blackness than had been the situation before the project was undertaken. It should be added that events independent of the summer project are likely to have influenced their opinions. For example, the uprising in the Watts section of Los Angeles in which thirty-four blacks were killed is likely to have had its effect on their attitudes and opinions.

The fact remains, however, that the enrollees in the summer project were mainly concerned about the daily issues of earning a livelihood and such long range interests as self-improvement. Political issues apparently played minor roles in their lives.

*   *   *

In evaluating the project at the end of summer, the youth whom it had been designed to serve expressed disappointment in that the project did not live up to their expectations. It will be recalled that these youth had looked to the project for personal improvement; they had expected it to assist the other youth in the area; and they had expressed the hope that it would improve the Harlem community. In each of these areas they reported that the project had failed to live up to their expectations. The greatest disappointment was registered insofar as community improvement was concerned. In this realm they felt that the project fell far short of its goal.

That is not to say that they do not attribute a measure of success to the project. Most of them thought it "somewhat useful," but in general their appraisal of its usefulness was tempered with realism. After all, how much could a ten-week project designed to contain a community do in changing the basic ills of that community? To expect more than moderate success in meeting the community's problems would have been unrealistic. Nevertheless, a vast majority of the enrollees indicated that should the occasion present itself, they would again participate. Such a finding is to be expected since in spite of its many problems and disappointments, they were able to earn salaries in excess of what they could have otherwise expected, had they been able to secure employment.

Although most of the youth expressed a willingness to participate in future projects, they readily listed their complaints. Invariably the most frequent complaints centered around delays in payroll procedures. After all, income had been their major motivation for participating. Payroll lists were to be turned in on Monday morning by supervisors for the preceding week, and enrollees were to be issued the checks on Friday. As often as not checks were delayed and when they finally arrived they were frequently in error. The complaints were understandable and parents of the youth were frequently as annoyed by such inefficiency as were the enrollees.

In addition to the payroll situation the youth complained about the over-all lack of efficiency in the project. Such situations as the late arrival of supplies, the inability to procure necessary supplies and equipment, and the lack of coordination were frequently listed as complaints. Finally, the youth complained about the difficulties they encountered with their supervisors and their fellow workers.

Conclusions

An attempt has been made to describe the youth whom the summer project was designed to serve. They were not in any way atypical for youth in Central Harlem. Recruitment took place on a first-come, first-served basis, and since the most destitute residents in the slums are less likely to have been aware of the existence of the project, the participants may not have represented the poorest families in the area. They went through a maze of confusion during the first few weeks and their tolerance of the constant ambiguity can probably be attributed to their desire to earn the above-average salaries they were paid. When given responsible tasks they worked diligently, frequently in excess of the contractual requirements. They talked freely about a variety of subjects, and one somehow began to feel that if the social conditions surrounding their lives were different, they would no doubt make significant contributions to the society. But the major impediment to such a realization is not that they have low verbal skills or that they do not score highly on intelligence tests. In American society they are black and accordingly they can look forward to being treated in a fashion commensurate with the low status that that designation carries. They learn early in life that for them to "make it" in American society some extraordinary set of circumstances must develop, and too few of these instances have occurred for them to have much hope. Most of them were probably average students in the schools they attended, and for most Americans this is sufficient to insure at least some reasonably comfortable "lower-middle-class" life. But they are not "most Americans" and the likelihood is that when they apply for employment, for some bizarre reason they will lack the proper qualifications for the job, and in the end they too will be relegated to the position of collecting "welfare" checks.

Not all of the youth in the project were typical Harlem teenagers or young adults. That so many of them managed to stay in school is a tribute to their persistence in the face of constant refusals to teach them. However, the project's administration made a decision to include as many of Harlem's youth in the project as possible regardless of their court records or the existence of personal pathologies or beliefs. Hence, among the youth described above were to be found those with criminal records, those addicted to narcotics, and those who are members of the Black Muslims.

In some cases, those individuals with serious problems of adjustment were given positions of responsibility and as a rule they performed these tasks well and began to understand their own personal problems. Perhaps the most general statement to be made about the youth in the summer project in the short period of ten weeks is that they succeeded in destroying many of the negative stereotypes which have been created about them by white Americans. The extraordinary thing was not that a few of them performed their tasks poorly, but that given the circumstances of their lives and of this project, that so many of them performed their responsibilities with such diligence and competence.

CHAPTER SIX

Project Uplift
and the Harlem Community

Introduction

An important aspect of any poverty project and one crucial to its success or failure is the impact it makes on the community in which it operates. In the case of PUL this impact came from a number of sources; the coverage of Project Uplift activities by the news media, both Harlem-based and city-wide, efforts by the public relations office of PUL itself to inform the community about the project, and certain special programs designed to involve or inform members of the larger community. In examining PUL's efforts along these lines one must ask questions about "public relations" carried on by a publicly supported program in the "war on poverty." In the literature produced by PUL during the summer the terms "public" relations and "community" relations were used interchangeably. In most publicly supported institutions and programs the term "community" relations is used since the connotations are less commercial. However, the methods, operations, and purposes are very similar to those used by commercial firms engaged in "public" relations. At the end of this chapter are recommended guidelines for public relations activities carried out by poverty projects.

The Community and Public Relations Department

In order to evaluate intelligently the public relations programs of Project Uplift, it seems sensible to look first at the structure

and operation of the department charged with this responsibility. There was no provision made for a public relations department in the initial proposal, and it, therefore, was the creation of the Project Coordinator with its responsibilities and
duties designated by him rather than by the Office of Economic
Opportunity. In a sense the operation of this department represented an experiment within federal projects of this nature. Project Uplift was fortunate in having as director of this department
an experienced community relations worker who also had the
ability to get from her co-workers considerable effort. The
general training function of PUL was not lost sight of in the
Community and Public Relations Department. Virtually all of
the enrollees were untrained and inexperienced in communication skills at the beginning of the summer, and it was necessary
to give them training in a variety of areas. Beyond a training and
practice ground for the enrollees the function of the department
was to provide informational and public relations material to all
enrollees and staff members, to professional representatives of
the mass media, and to the general Harlem community.

Perhaps the most important instrument for relating to both
the PUL enrollees and staff and the general public was the
weekly eight-page newspaper *Newsbriefs*. This paper was written,
edited, and set up exclusively by enrollees, although the actual
printing was done by an outside firm. Professional advice and
consultation were provided by the director and several other
staff members with newspaper experience. Nine issues of *Newsbriefs* appeared during the summer with a total run of 145,000
copies. Seventeen enrollees made up the staff of the paper. As
might be expected working hours were somewhat irregular, with
long overtime periods being necessary to meet publishing deadlines. Most deadlines were met during the summer and the newspaper was looked forward to with considerable anticipation by
the enrollees and staff of the project. Contents included coverage of all PUL work programs, interviews with enrollees and
staff, feature stories, and editorials by members of the newspaper staff. There were inevitably a certain number of hortatory
statements by officials of both HARYOU and Project Uplift, but
these were kept to a minimum. Critical statements and comments by enrollees were not absent. From reading the "Letters

to the Editor," one could gain some insight into the feelings of enrollees about such sensitive matters as meeting the payroll deadline. Several highly critical drama reviews appeared after the Black Arts Theatre was funded and began to present its plays. Although praising the caliber of acting and the professional production of the plays, the *Newsbriefs* drama critic (an enrollee) criticized the Jones plays for fostering tension between blacks and whites. *Newsbriefs* contained typographical errors, misplaced captions under photographs, and in some instances poor writing. But all of these problems decreased as the summer progressed, giving proof that the enrollees involved were learning from the experience. The newspapers were distributed by a special unit of the Community and Public Relations Department. Certain distributing points were identified, including churches and community centers as well as stores and shops throughout Harlem.

Closely related to *Newsbriefs* but separate in structure was the Art Department. It was responsible for preparing all visual materials, posters, fliers, leaflets, as well as cartoons and drawings which appeared in *Newsbriefs.* The posters and fliers announced programs such as the Harlem Olympics, the PUL Art Gallery, and the Final Parade and Festival Day. It was also fulfilling a training function for enrollees assigned to it, since the section was supervised by a professional commercial artist. Approximately 80,000 posters, fliers and leaflets were produced by the Art Department and distributed throughout the Harlem community.

Frequently the size of an activity or the importance attached to it in an original plan bears no relationship to the impact of this activity when it is in operation. Almost as an afterthought a professional dancer, LaRoque Bey, was hired by Project Uplift, and fourteen girls between the ages of fourteen and eighteen without previous experience or training in dance were assigned to him. In spite of some initial objection by the girls to the discipline and hard work forced on them, this group, known as the LaRoque Bey Dancers, developed considerable skill and performed before a number of groups in Harlem during the latter weeks of the summer. During the Final Parade and Festival Day in Central Park their performance attracted more spectators than any other demonstration. The impact on the Harlem community, although difficult to measure, was certainly considerable. The LaRoque Bey Dancers received newspaper coverage in *Newsbriefs*, Harlem newspapers, and in the general mass media.

In addition to the projects described above, the Community and Public Relations Department had the responsibility of planning and directing Project Uplift's share of the Final Parade and Festival Day. With limited resources and unskilled personnel this department must be given a major share of the credit for Project Uplift's image in Harlem. It would be encouraging to report that many or even some of the enrollees who went through this intensive training program went on to obtain positions in the field of communications. Unfortunately in this area of work as in all others, there was almost no follow-up and very few, if any, enrollees involved with the Community and Public Relations Department obtained full or part-time jobs in this field. Elsewhere in the book are more detailed comments on this special problem of job placement and follow-up in short-term poverty projects.

The News Media

Coverage of Project Uplift activities by Harlem media (radio and newspapers) was extensive and in general quite favorable during the course of the summer. Interviews were held with the Project Coordinator and other staff members of Project Uplift. Photographs appeared regularly in the *Amsterdam News* depicting the various activities of the enrollees. The clear impression carried by these media was that of a busy, purposeful and generally successful summer program. The one exception to this was several reports concerning the difficulty of paying enrollees on time. The coverage provided by city-wide newspapers, radio, and television was also very favorable during the course of the summer. It was not until September and October when the question was raised about missing and/or commingled funds that articles and reports of a more critical nature appeared. The general impression given during the summer was of a program with some administrative problems because of its size and the speed with which it had been developed, but, in general, of a program serving the needs of the youth of Central Harlem with some effectiveness. It was in the identification of Project Uplift with HARYOU by the media that some of the problems of HARYOU vis-a-vis Project Uplift first came to light. Permanent HARYOU staff members became upset when Project Uplift was not clearly and continually identified as a special project of HARYOU. While on the other hand PUL staff members were concerned when Project Uplift was treated as only one among many projects which HARYOU was operating at the time. It should be noted here that during the entire summer the public relations departments of both HARYOU and Project Uplift were producing releases for the media with virtually no coordination or cooperation. For example, Project Uplift very soon after its inception developed the weekly newspaper, *Newsbriefs*, which was shortly followed by a HARYOU paper. Some of the feeling between the two staffs was undoubtedly inevitable. But certainly a more coordinated or at least non-conflicting system of informing the general public should have been worked out.

Special Community Related Programs

Several special programs were developed during the course of the summer for the purpose of informing and involving the broader Harlem community.

Black Arts Theatre

Clearly the most controversial of these community oriented programs was the Black Arts Repertory Theatre. This program, begun about the middle of the summer, had as its purpose developing and conducting programs in theater, as well as music, poetry, art, and photography. The Black Arts Theatre had existed for some time in the Harlem community under the direction of playwright-poet LeRoi Jones. The staff of both Project Uplift and HARYOU were not unaware of Jones' Black Nationalist position since he had never made any secret of this and indeed had made Black Nationalism a central theme in most of his creative work. It was felt, however, that only someone like Jones, who then lived and worked in the Harlem community, and who had a theater group already in existence, could move into operation in the time available. Portable theatrical equipment was purchased by Project Uplift, turned over to the Black Arts Theatre and used to present a series of street-corner productions at a number of locations in Central Harlem. Enrollees in Project Uplift were actors, stagehands, and in some cases, stage designers and assistant directors. The level of the productions was good and they were well received by the audiences in attendance. The controversy surrounding the Black Arts Theatre arose out of the subject matter of the plays produced. They dealt with racial conflict and tried to foster a "positive" identification for black youth by portraying whites as outsmarted, overpowered, defeated, and in some cases, killed by blacks. Also the controversy arose after the fact when some reports of the plays were picked up by the city press and copies of several scripts got into the hands of senators and congressmen who apparently planned to use them as ammunition in their fight against the entire "war on poverty." Possibly, the controversy raised by these plays was out of proportion to the seriousness of the project itself. It may indeed have been poor tactics to present plays featuring racial conflict when financed by a federal project, and yet if there was to be any theater in the summer crash program, the Black Arts Theatre was the only group at that time equipped to provide it.

Painting and photography were encouraged. The Black Arts building served as an exhibit gallery and in addition sidewalk exhibits of art were held in a variety of locations throughout Harlem. These shows also appeared to be popular with the community and many residents seemed impressed with both the quality and the fact that the work was done by Harlem youth.

The Black Arts Theatre also conducted a series of group discussions for the enrollees involved in its program. These discussions seemed to be in part therapeutic, providing an opportunity for the young people to air grievances and to discuss problems, but in addition broader social questions were covered. In spite of the fact that no professional group leaders were involved these sessions were extremely popular with the enrollees. It is interesting to note that there was no evidence of any attempt to "brainwash" the enrollees in terms of Black Nationalism, even though this ideology was strongly expressed in the plays presented by the group.

Harlem Olympics

The Harlem Olympics was a contest in track and field events designed to encourage these activities among the youth of Harlem, and in addition to provide a spectator sport for parents and other Harlem residents. Local and regional meets were held throughout Harlem during the early part of the summer, with the finals, the actual Olympics, held on August 28 at Downing Stadium on Randalls Island. A variety of organizations combined to sponsor this program including churches, local community organizations, and prominent black athletes. Some 300 young people (not limited to enrollees in PUL) participated in the final event. The program itself was well organized and very smoothly operated. Attendance by parents of youngsters participating and other adults in the Harlem community, however, was almost completely lacking. Certainly one problem in involving the community in this program was the location of the event since Randalls Island is not easily accessible to Harlem residents. In addition to the lack of spectators, it had been announced and publicized that several prominent community leaders, including Livingston Wingate, would be present. When none of these leaders put in an appearance, disappointment on the part of the participants was clearly evident. Considerable responsibility must be laid to the failure of PUL and HARYOU to cooperate on publicity efforts. After the Olympics had taken place there was considerable competitive maneuvering between PUL and HARYOU for credit in planning and developing the event.

Art Gallery

Because of the magnitude of Project Uplift and the size of the operational staff, additional space was rented for the project at 45 West 125th Street. This large empty building had been a furniture store and contained thousands of square feet of floor space on four levels, plus sixty feet of window space fronting on Harlem's main street. The public relations department of Project Uplift decided to use part of the first floor as an art gallery to show Harlem residents works by indigenous professional artists.

Few Harlemites can afford to own an original work of art, and few venture downtown to visit galleries where these works would be shown. Consequently they were quite unaware of the dozens of talented professional artists living in their midst. A member of PUL's community and public relations department contacted several artists in Harlem, who in turn contacted others, and the gallery was set up by the fourth week of the project. A new show was presented each week. This program was judged to be so successful both by the artists involved and by the community that it was continued for some time by HARYOU after the end of the summer. During the summer approximately 10,000 Harlem residents had visited the exhibitions. PUL enrollees were utilized in manning the gallery, in obtaining and hanging the works of art, and in seeing that they were returned after each weekly show. The impact of this program on Harlem clearly outweighed the relatively small amount of effort and coordination it took to set it up.

Final Parade and Festival

As the summer progressed the staff of Project Uplift began to realize that one serious problem could end their crash program. On the last Friday enrollees would work, hopefully receive their pay checks, and that would be the end of it. As an attempt to overcome this sharp psychological break a final day of special activities was conceived. It eventually consisted of a parade through Harlem with floats and marching units provided by all of the program vehicles of PUL and other programs in HARYOU. The parade was followed by a festival in Central Park with demonstrations consisting of a variety of exhibits and productions staged by groups of enrollees from the various programs of PUL. It included art exhibits, poetry readings, several dance troupes, dramatic productions, demonstrations of reading classes, and other features. The second half of the festival program consisted of a combination of performers (professional as well as PUL enrollees) and the inevitable series of speeches delivered by community dignitaries and leaders of HARYOU. From a public or community relations point of view this Final Parade and Festival must be judged a success. An estimated crowd of 40,000 to 50,000 people observed the parade through

Harlem, while another 15,000 to 20,000 attended the festival in Central Park. The planning phase for the Parade and Festival was made particularly difficult by a failure to agree early on the sponsorship for the day. The leaders of PUL, since they originated the idea and had as their purpose the desire to end their crash program on a high note, wished to be the sole sponsors of the day. Some board members and executives of HARYOU on the other hand seemed fearful that HARYOU would not get the publicity and credit that it deserved if PUL had its way. After literally weeks of wrangling during which no plans could be made, a compromise solution was reached in which the parade was sponsored by HARYOU and included among its thirty floats and marching units representatives from programs in addition to those of Project Uplift. The festival on the other hand was limited to PUL. Both the festival and the parade, however, were planned and executed by PUL staff. Press coverage for this event was highly favorable and extensive. To some extent this day seemed to accomplish the purpose for which it was designed, that of ending the summer project on a high note.

These programs were all designed at least in part to serve the wider community through both informing them about Project Uplift and involving them as participants or spectators in one or another phase of the program. It is quite clear, however, that actually all of the program vehicles in PUL had some impact on the Harlem community. A building being painted, a vest-pocket park being built, a day camp being operated by enrollees—all made some contribution to the over-all impact of PUL on the residents of Harlem.

Impact on the Community

Assessing accurately the impact of a complex summer program like Project Uplift on a community like Harlem is an extremely difficult job. That some impact was made is reasonably clear. Many Harlem residents came into contact with PUL enrollees painting a building, directing a recreation program on a street or in a playground, observed the enrollment trucks complete with signs and posters that were located in various parts of Harlem in the early part of the summer, and if they read local newspapers or listened to radio stations, were certainly made aware of PUL's existence through these media. But how many people in Central Harlem were aware of Project Uplift's existence, what did they know about it, and how did both the ordinary citizen of Harlem and local community leaders come to judge Project Uplift's effectiveness? There are several sources of information for estimating PUL's impact on Harlem.

Community Survey Section

In the initial proposal for Project Uplift the community survey section was placed within the community and public relations department, and was designed to have two functions. First, enrollees would be trained to identify neighborhood needs in Harlem and evaluate the impact of PUL on the community. And secondly, these enrollees would be employed in block organizations and tenant groups to assist and develop maximum resident participation. Some 125 enrollees of the associate category were involved in the project working under five supervisors. It is unfortunate that as potentially useful and important as the above goals were, no trained social scientist or researcher was assigned to supervise or consult with this group. Indeed during the course of the summer the day-to-day work of the community survey section was one of the more elusive elements in the summer project. At the close of the summer, however, a report was submitted describing the work carried out by this section.

In the area of housing the community survey section assisted individual tenants in making housing complaints to the rent and rehabilitation office. Follow-up procedures were initiated to make sure that action had been taken. The enrollees working in the area of housing had a series of conferences with the city rent and rehabilitation office which were attended also by representatives of the United Block Association. An information sheet on housing was prepared and distributed to residents in several Harlem neighborhoods.

"Negro Heritage" discussion groups were initiated for enrollees in the community survey section. A number of enrollees were assigned to do research on Afro-American history and then to report their findings to the group. All of the enrollees were given assigned reading and were required to read for four hours each week. This was the only activity of the community survey section which did not reach out into the Harlem community at large. The rationale for including it in the work of the section was apparently that young black men and women who better understand their heritage would be more effective and make a better impact on the community they were trying to influence.

A very interesting project was begun about the middle of the summer dealing with commercial exploitation of Harlem residents by local merchants. Some comparisons were made between prices in Harlem and those in downtown stores on food, clothing and furniture. To no one's great surprise in many areas prices in Harlem were higher. It is unfortunate that because of its late start this study which seemed to have been well thought out was not completed.

The fourth activity of the community survey section was identifying unregistered voters in the Harlem community. This survey consisted of approximately 1,140 interviews with Harlem residents during which they were urged to register and were given voting information. In addition to finding out whether or not the interviewees were registered, they were also questioned about PUL. They were asked the question, "Have you heard of HARYOU's summer program, Project Uplift?" Some 918 responded "yes," 222 "no." When asked what PUL programs and activities they had heard about the replies were as follows: day camps, 537; beautification, 278; vest-pocket parks, 171; remedial reading, 133; other, 117.

When asked where they had heard about PUL, the two most often mentioned sources were the *Amsterdam News* (the most influential weekly newspaper in Harlem), and "from relatives and friends in the project." Other important sources included the two Harlem radio stations and the *New York Daily News.* When those who had heard of PUL were asked if in their opinion it was doing a good job, two-thirds said it was, with only twenty-six out of 916 saying it was doing a poor, or very poor job. As interesting as the above results are, however, their general usefulness must be seriously questioned. In a report submitted to the Project Coordinator, the community survey section stated that the interviews were derived from "random sampling." However, no sampling procedures were used at all. Interviewers simply talked with people on the streets and rang doorbells with no defined pattern. As a result it is impossible to generalize about the Harlem community from the above figures. They show only what 1100 people in Harlem did know and think about PUL. None of the five supervisors who directed the work of the 125 enrollees had any background in survey research and since they seemed to be working almost entirely in the field, the control exercised over them by the director of the community and public relations department was very slight. It is certainly to be regretted that this group of 125 very dedicated and active enrollees did not have their work better structured. Nevertheless this group was clearly the part of PUL which came into most direct and sustained contact with Harlem residents not otherwise involved. "Finding a voice in the community" was given in the original proposal as the justification for the community survey section. This rather vague and indeed ambiguous guideline might in part be blamed for the way in which their work was carried out.

Leaders of Local Community Organizations

Another method of assessing the impact of PUL on the Harlem community was to question the leaders of local community organizations who were involved in some way with PUL. More neighborhood organizations were subcontracted to the Associated Community Teams (responsible for all day camps) than to HANA, the Urban League, or HAC combined. Two-thirds of the neighborhood organizations in PUL were churches. These varied from large well-established institutions which had deep historical roots in the community to small "store-front" churches not affiliated with any national denomination. Many of the larger organizations had operated summer programs before the summer of 1965. By the end of the fifth week, of thirty-eight neighborhood organizations which could be identified as having become part of the summer project, 40 per cent reported that they had received supplies, 60 per cent had received staff in the form of PUL enrollees attached to their activity, and about 20 per cent reported that they had as yet received no help from PUL.

By the end of the summer, of forty-six neighborhood organization leaders interviewed, all had received assistance from PUL in one or more of their summer programs. Almost all had received supplies of some kind. All received enrollees, while sixteen were helped in program planning, and twelve received financial help of a kind other than supplies. The kinds of programs for which they received assistance ranged over the usual programs associated with day camps. Arts and crafts, recreation, drama and theater, black heritage, and remedial reading were most commonly assisted. When asked how satisfied they were with the assistance received from PUL, the directors of these neighborhood organizations responded as follows:

Highly satisfied	14
Moderately satisfied	24
Moderately dissatisfied	5
Highly dissatisfied	2
No answer	1
Total organizations	46

All of the neighborhood organizations felt that a program resembling the activities of the summer project should be expanded and carried out on a year-round basis.

The number of enrollees assigned to neighborhood organizations varied from one or two attached to a very small day camp, to seventy or eighty attached to the summer program of a large well-established church. Most neighborhood organizations used some enrollees in supervisory capacities and seemed to be generally satisfied with their performance. There were in fact few complaints about the performance of PUL enrollees and the overwhelming majority of neighborhood organization leaders would participate in a similar program if offered in future summers. They identify unemployment and economic conditions, low educational standards, and apathy in the community as the three major problems facing Harlem, and 80 per cent felt that PUL had contributed in some measure to resolving these problems.

Day-Camp Families Interviewed

The largest single component of PUL was the day-camp program directed by the Associated Community Teams. It involved slightly over half of the enrollees who in turn served approximately 17,000 Harlem children. These children represented a significant contact with the broader Harlem community. To get some measure of the impact of PUL on this part of the general public of Harlem, 300 interviews were conducted with families of children attending day camps sponsored by PUL. In general terms these 300 Harlem families appeared to be fairly representative of the larger Harlem community. A number of the interviewed, however, refused to answer questions relating to income and education (a standard problem for survey research in a slum community) making a rigorous comparison impossible. Only one out of three of those interviewed spontaneously replied that he had heard of either HARYOU or PUL. Another third indicated that they were not aware of any other activity besides the day-camp program in which their child or children were enrolled. As might be expected those families higher in socio-economic level were more familiar with the summer project. In those families where the head of the household was unemployed, knowledge of HARYOU or PUL was rarely found. All interviewees who did not mention spontaneously that they had heard of HARYOU or PUL were then asked directly if they had heard of Project Uplift, the special summer project of HARYOU. When asked in this way three out of four responded that they did recognize the names. Of those who recognized the names, however, only one out of six went on to say that he knew PUL was providing work for young people. The most frequent program mentioned was, of course, day camps. The second most frequently mentioned was building repairs. Other programs were mentioned by only a very small percentage of those interviewed. Those who had heard of the summer project were also asked to evaluate the job being done that summer. The majority responded that in their opinion HARYOU was doing a very good job. Practically no one felt the summer activities were "poor" or "very poor." In summary, about four out of five of those interviewed were at least familiar with the name HARYOU or Project Uplift, but relatively few could identify the specific programs or types of activities that were being carried out. Of this same four-fifths, a substantial majority indicated that they were favorably impressed with the summer project.

Community Leaders Interviewed

Another method of assessing the impact of PUL on the community in Harlem was to find out what prominent community leaders thought about the project. Certainly these individuals would from their positions as leaders influence the attitude of the general public both within and outside Harlem. Among the community leaders identified were a newspaper editor, two leaders of prominent community service organizations, two elected public officials, three leaders of civil rights organizations, and two widely known radical political dissidents. From this list of titles it is clear that there was a wide divergence of political points of view. In spite of this divergence there were a number of opinions shared by all of these community leaders. All of them reacted favorably to the fact that the federal government seemed to be taking a greater interest in Harlem and was willing to finance a fairly massive summer program like Project Uplift. On the other hand almost all of these leaders felt that a summer crash program by itself could not accomplish very much. After the summer is over, "the schools are the same, the tenements and the police are the same, drugs are still here." Another leader said, "Project Uplift definitely does not guarantee heat and hot water in the home. The same youth who is uplifted in the summer will freeze in the winter. There should be equal concern for keeping the youth hot in the winter as well as cool in the summer."

Several community leaders complained that the project was only a pacifier and did not deal with the real and basic problems of Harlem. All agreed that there was a need to institute a massive program on a year-round basis. They also agreed on the importance of extending the age limits to include not just young people but adults and elderly Harlem residents as well. Suggestions for this massive year-round program included job training, recreation programs, Afro-American and African heritage programs, and work-study programs for school age youngsters and drop outs. Several community leaders felt that the project did not reach the right youngsters. "Many of the more disaffected youth in Harlem viewed the project as an attempt by 'the man' to buy them off. Most of these young people did not join the program." Another almost universal complaint about the project was its involvement in politics. Several community leaders said that staff jobs in anti-poverty projects in Harlem were given on the basis of political friendship. Another leader said that he could only describe the summer project as a "political football." One interviewee long active in community service work in Harlem felt that programs like PUL would be more effective if set up independently or funneled directly to local community agencies throughout Harlem. There was considerable criticism of some of the work assigned to the enrollees. "Sure, the PUL youngsters have jobs, but they're not jobs for the future. PUL has failed to have training oriented jobs. PUL gave them something to hang onto over the summer and has left them nothing." Finally, all of the community leaders interviewed expressed themselves on the relationship between PUL and the absence of riots during the summer. The opinions ranged from crediting Project Uplift with a great deal of influence for the "quiet summer" to doubting that the project had any influence at all.

In summary, then, these community leaders seemed to feel that the existence of PUL and the federal interest which it represented were good. They also agreed that more sustained year-round effort was necessary. Beyond this agreement there were diversions of opinion about the effectiveness of various parts of the program, the way it was organized, the young people involved, and the role of PUL in deterring riots in Harlem.

Public Relations and Poverty Projects: Some Guidelines

Public relations and poverty, what could be further apart than these two terms? The first connotes Madison Avenue, gray flannel suits, lies and half-lies for the purpose of "promoting an image," and a faint aroma of all around dishonesty. This seems quite removed from a poverty project for the employment of youth in a slum like Harlem. And, of course, it is. But when one looks closely at such a project it becomes apparent that to be truly successful it needs the support and encouragement of the community in which it is operating, as well as a real and sustained effort by everyone working for it. This means some effort to inform, to persuade and even to "sell" the importance of a project to the larger community.

There are obvious dangers in developing "public relations" for a poverty program. Most obvious is dishonesty; assertions can be made about the activities and the success of those activities which are simply not true. A public relations program may also be used for other ends than that for which it was originally designed. It may be used to promote the personal image of the project director, the public relations director, or some other prominent community figure who has perhaps been influential in creating the project. Another danger, particularly from the point of view of the federal government, is that dishonest and exaggerated public relations may disguise failures even from the people working in the project and from those in Washington responsible for its operation. For these reasons the federal government has not authorized the use of any federal money for strictly public relations activity.

There are certainly no easy or pat answers to the above dangers but we believe that the following guidelines adhered to faithfully would go some way to assuring a public relations program that would be both honest and useful in furthering the purposes of the particular project of which it would be a part.

1. The first and most crucially important guideline for a poverty public relations program is that of absolute honesty. All facts and figures, estimates, predictions, and summaries must be as honest and as accurate as possible. This is not to say that in all cases and at all times a particular problem in one sector of the program need be given the same emphasis as a more successful part, but simply that whatever is presented to the public must represent what actually exists in the program.

2. In conducting interviews and presenting personalities to the public the emphasis should be on the indigenous members of

the community, local volunteers and those on the "firing line" rather than on the professional who may not be a member of the community. Emphasis on the personalities of project directors, politicians, community leaders, or other prominent figures should be avoided. Project Uplift's public relations program was reasonably good in this respect. Many interviews with comments from the enrollees appeared in *Newsbriefs* compared with few interviews and statements by high level staff members and community leaders.

3. The target for a poverty public relations program should be the community in which it is operating and not the city-wide or national news media. It is very tempting to try to capture city-wide or nation-wide attention for a particular project. Indeed sometimes this is unavoidable. But the main business of public relations for a poverty project should be to inform, involve, and convince the local community. The public relations department of Project Uplift adhered quite well to this guideline. PUL was discussed in the city media and occasionally in the national media but most of the energies of the department were directed toward the local community.

4. An important objective for poverty public relations should be to develop a feeling about the project in the community to a point where community members will express themselves freely and frankly. The establishment of this dialogue should assist the project in achieving its goals. During the life of PUL there was not time to develop adequately this phase of the public relations program. There were frequent comments and criticisms by enrollees and staff members, but few comments by Harlem residents outside of the project.

5. In every poverty project which has a public relations component, there should be a separate program of evaluation independent of the project administration. This program of evaluation would be able to bring to the project director's attention any discrepancies between the public relations statements and the actual situation. To do this the evaluation must be conducted on a day-to-day or week-to-week basis during the life of the project as well as at its conclusion. The existence of such a program of evaluation would also serve as a source of information for accurate facts and figures to be used for public rela-

tions. The structure suggested above did exist in Project Uplift although the public relations department rarely used the information available from the evaluators.

6. In any poverty project involving the employment, training, or voluntary activities of the poor, the training function of a public relations program should be equally as important as its communications function. This means that the public relations staff must not be made up of outside professionals brought in to sell the project but rather of community members who would learn communications skills under the direction of a trained supervisor. If the training function is made equal in importance to communications, it seems likely that the federal government as well as other government agencies would be less reluctant to authorize the use of public monies for this purpose. One of the best features of Project Uplift's public relations was that the training element predominated. Untrained young people from Harlem were utilized in all phases and at many levels of the program.

CHAPTER SEVEN

Project Uplift:
Major Strengths and Weaknesses

Introduction

In a summer project involving hundreds of staff members, thousands of enrollees and serving tens of thousands in the community there will be a great range in the quality of performance. This was certainly true of Project Uplift. Some things worked well, some were partially successful, while other components of the project failed completely. In this chapter the efforts which were made in all areas of Project Uplift are described and judged with emphasis on the main work programs since these were the heart of the project. Some persistent weaknesses and major strengths of the summer program are also considered. Finally, what should be extracted from this experience and applied to future projects in Harlem and in other urban slum communities across the nation is identified.

The Programs

The Day-Camp Program

The day-camp program had two general objectives: first, to provide structured educational and recreational activities for children and young people in central Harlem; and secondly, to provide an enriching work experience for the enrollees involved in the program. In pursuing these general objectives the day-camp program attempts to achieve certain, more specific goals for the enrollees. These are reported by the directors of this program including a heightened self-image, a higher motivation for better education and life expectations, a sense of pride in community, an appreciation of the importance of working with young children, good work habits, and experience in the handling of money (the first for many enrollees, at least in the form of a regular weekly salary). Sixty-eight day camps were supervised by Associated Community Teams and employed Project Uplift enrollees in teaching and supervisory capacities. As might be expected the programs varied widely. One of the largest, the Abyssinian Baptist Church, had a well-organized and varied program including activities and training in music, dancing, dramatic arts, swimming, and handicrafts, in addition to special field trips and a series of educational films. Some 318 Harlem youngsters were registered in this day camp with seventeen PUL enrollees assigned to work with the regular church staff.

The Citizen's Care Day Center involved 381 Harlem children between the ages of five and thirteen. Its program focused on arts and crafts. It did conduct, however, additional programs in remedial reading and cultural enrichment with an emphasis on Afro-American heritage. A majority (41 out of 68) of the day camps were sponsored by churches. It is interesting to note that their programs did not differ significantly from those sponsored by secular agencies. Although there was considerable variation in emphasis, practically all of them included games, arts and crafts, black history, remedial reading and field trips. These field trips took thousands of Harlem children to local libraries, zoos, museums, the World's Fair, beaches, and in several cases picnics in nearby parks. Some 1500 Harlem youth received instruction in swimming programs and about 600 participated in a free lunch program which a number of day camps sponsored.

One thing which must be kept in mind when evaluating the effectiveness of the day-camp program as part of Project Uplift is that many churches and local community agencies had on their own initiative operated day camps during previous summers. This meant in a sense that PUL's day-camp program was plugged into an on-going and established summer activity. For many of the day camps then, PUL's participation provided the opportunity to extend without cost additional services to the youngsters and to increase teaching and supervisory staff by using PUL enrollees. The task of coordinating and organizing this part of the summer project was, in important ways, an easier one. The supervisors were not starting from scratch or attempting to introduce a program which was unfamiliar to Harlem residents. Part of the success achieved by the day-camp program must be attributed to local ministers, block association leaders, and other members of the Harlem community who had previously organized and developed day-camp programs using their own financial and staff resources.

In spite of the general success of this program the day camps did experience a number of problems, many of which afflicted other parts of PUL. Most important among these were delays in pay for both the enrollees and supervisors. These delays clearly affected the morale of the PUL workers assigned to day camps, particularly since staff members paid by the local church or neighborhood organizations received salary checks on time.

Some difficulties resulting from confusion in the line of authority between the staff of PUL, the staff of ACT and the local organization staff developed. At the beginning of the day-camp program, ACT hired both supervisors and enrollees without first clearing through the PUL personnel department. As a result a number of duplicate assignments were made to various day camps. A closely related problem involved the inspection of day camps by supervisors or investigators from a number of different agencies. ACT itself employed supervisors. PUL's program training and development section also sent out field personnel. HARYOU employed a field liaison staff, and finally, the evaluation office of PUL sent investigators into the field to observe the activities of the day camps. Although most of these visitors tried to conduct themselves so as to interfere as little as possible with the program of the day camp, there was confusion and justified resentment on the part of camp personnel toward these supervisors from other parts of the project. Although some of this duplication was inevitable it points up the importance of clearly drawn lines of authority and responsibility and the need to encourage initiative and responsibility on the local level.

Another problem which severely hampered a number of the day camps was the delay in receiving needed supplies. Many day-camp programs found themselves without supplies for as long as three or four weeks and either had to spend their own money or improvise with free materials. The major components of many day-camp programs were arts and crafts, music, dance, and remedial reading, activities for which special equipment and supplies were essential.

Another weakness of PUL affecting the day-camp program was the lack of adequate orientation and training for both enrollees and supervisors. Because of the crash nature of the project and because sufficient provision for a phasing-in period was not in the original proposal, most enrollees and supervisors had to get what training they could while on the job and actually working with children in the day camps.

In spite of these serious problems there were several indications that the day-camp program performed a worthwhile service to the Harlem community. There was, for example, an extremely low rate of absenteeism among the enrollees. In no week of the summer did the rate reach one per cent. The supervisors of ACT were themselves, for the most part, satisfied with the program. In their reports submitted to the coordinator of Project Uplift, they indicated a generally high level of satisfaction. The great majority (88 per cent) of enrollees who worked in the day camps rated the activity as having been a successful one. This was a higher figure than for most of the other activities. The parents of children served by the day-camp program were asked how well the camps had done their job. An overwhelming majority felt that the camps had done very well in "keeping the children busy and out of trouble" and also "motivating interest in new things." Some 47 per cent of the parents said that the day camps had done very well in "instilling race pride in the children" and 41 per cent praised the camps for "helping the children improve their reading skills."

Residential Summer Camps

The objectives of the residential summer camp program directed by Associated Community Teams were in general the same as those for the day-camp program. The difference between the two was that the residential camps were specifically designed to serve children from families of the lowest income brackets and thus provide an experience which obviously would not otherwise have been available to them. Responsibility for this program was assigned to two neighborhood organizations, the Church of the Master, and the Harlem Parents' Committee. A total of five summer camps participated in this program. Three of the camps were in Minnesota and Colorado. Rather limited information is available about their activities. PUL's participation in these three camps consisted of paying the costs for a certain number of youngsters to attend. No enrollees or PUL supervisors were involved in camp activities. One of them involved the integration by ten boys from Harlem of a previously all-white camp. This experiment was apparently successful. Camp Patterson in Lake Ariel, Pennsylvania, was the one residential camp staffed and supervised by PUL personnel. It operated a specialized program for emotionally disturbed youth. This camping experience apparently developed a high level of participation and good morale on the part of both the youngsters from Harlem and the staff serving them. One unanswered question of course for all of the residential camps was how much did this experience carry over into and affect the lives of the youngsters after their return to central Harlem. Since there was no provision in Project Uplift for any follow-up research, this question must remain unanswered.

Three-quarters of the parents of these youth reported that the program had served its function very well in "organizing games and athletics" and "seeing that the children had fun." Over half of the parents reported that the residential camps did very well in "making the children proud of being Negroes," "developing interest in new things," "improving the children's health," and "teaching self-discipline." In a more limited sense and based on much more limited evidence the residential camp program was also a successful PUL activity. The same qualification entered for the day-camp program must also be entered here. Except for Camp Patterson the residential camps had been a regular summer feature of the Church of the Master. Here also PUL was attaching itself to an on-going program in the Harlem community.

Athletic Workshops

The objectives of the athletic workshop program as stated in the original proposal included providing a directed, supervised athletic experience for community youth; enrollees were to learn recreation skills to lead and direct games, to understand child growth and development, and to develop a sense of being effective, contributing, responsible individuals in the service of others. To achieve these objectives it was anticipated that enrollees would lead and direct basketball, softball, and football teams as well as track and field events. Athletic workshops were located at approximately thirty-three sites and were divided into five administrative districts. The program included forty-five basketball teams competing on levels ranging from junior high school through college. Track and field activities included five district track meets with the final Harlem Olympic Meet held at Randalls Island, August 28. Thirty softball teams were organized on both the intermediate and junior level. In addition to organizing the above teams and special events, enrollees were added to the staff of already existing summer programs, especially in those community agencies that would have been unable to offer extensive athletics without this additional personnel. Some 211 enrollees and fourteen supervisors served in this program. The director of athletic workshops reported that his program reached 10,000 youngsters in central Harlem.

The major problem for the athletic workshops was the delay in receiving supplies and equipment. The first athletic equipment supplied by Project Uplift was distributed to the athletic workshops on July 27th in the fifth week of the summer program. Because of this delay supervisors were forced to introduce games and activities which did not involve the use of equipment.

One additional problem that must be mentioned in connection with the athletic workshops is that of the salary range for the enrollees vs. the salary range for playground and athletic supervisors in programs sponsored by New York City or private agencies. For an eight-week summer $200 is a better than average salary for this kind of work. Enrollees at the assistant level were making $400 for the summer while associates were making $800 for a ten-week period. One must ask what psychological problems will arise when a youngster who had received $400 or $800 in a poverty project applies for a regular position and is offered $200.

Building Repairs

The building repairs program supervised by the Urban League of Greater New York was designed to contribute to several objectives. Municipal facilities would be improved, residential structures would be renovated, the enrollees would learn how to handle simple construction tools and materials, read and interpret plans and specifications, take directions from supervisors and other elementary work skills. In addition it was expected that residential participation in local organizations would be increased and that the self-concept and sense of identity of enrollees would be enhanced. The program was organized around work crews which received various assignments during the course of the summer. Building improvements were limited to clean-up, minor repairs, and painting. There was a total of 465 enrollees and twenty-eight supervisors involved in the building repairs program.

Of particular and crucial importance to building repairs was the delay in delivery of needed supplies. Work crews were held up in some cases for days because they did not have hammers, saws, paint, paint brushes, and other basic equipment. The director of this program complained bitterly about the number of liaison people who visited the work sites interviewing supervisors and crew members. These liaison personnel came from several different departments in Project Uplift and according to reports from individuals in the building repairs program they hindered the work.

This program vehicle got off to a particularly late start with no enrollees being assigned to it until July 15th. Delays in paying enrollees and supervisors and inaccuracies in the amount were serious problems which seemed to affect morale. One additional setback to building repairs was that until the beginning of August, HARYOU tried to insist on contracts being written between the Urban League and any local organization, institution, or private individual for whom building repairs were done. The delay involved in preparing these contracts resulted in virtually no work being accomplished until the first week of August. This policy was changed in August and as a result toward the end of the summer all crews were busy and many requests for repairs had to be turned down because of lack of time and personnel. Approximately fifty different building repair jobs were completed and ten were in progress when the summer project ended. In spite of the delay in starting the actual work, this program must be judged to have been moderately successful.

Remedial Reading

Remedial reading was given a prominent place in the original proposal for Project Uplift. The program was assigned to a Director of Remedial Reading who was on the PUL coordinator's staff and who was directly responsible to the project coordinator. Central among the many listed objectives of the remedial reading program was correcting deficiencies in reading skills and abilities, fostering growth in basic comprehensive abilities, word meaning, thought units, sentence sense, paragraphs, total selection, instruction in use of reference materials, and improving the reading level of enrollees through teaching reading to younger children.

Twenty remedial reading centers were established throughout central Harlem. These centers were in operation daily from 9 A.M. to 4 P.M., and served 1200 youth ranging in age from six to nineteen years. In addition to the remedial reading centers related program activities were established which included inservice training for remedial reading teachers and testing enrollees in the summer program for reading level. Because of a delay in delivery of reading supplies, preparing substitute material for use during the first five weeks was included. Ten supervisors and seventy-seven enrollees were employed in this program. The original plan was to use all of the enrollees assigned to this project as remedial reading instructors to work with younger children. However, the reading level for a number of enrollees was found to be so low that this plan was modified. Those enrollees at an extremely low reading level were assigned to a work study program which included a good deal of required reading and the preparation of compositions. The failure to foresee the possibility of enrollees with low reading levels and to take this into account in the design of the program was a serious oversight.

Remedial reading, too, faced a delay in receiving supplies and materials. Until the fifth week enrollees and supervisors were forced to bring work books, textbooks, paper, and pencils from their homes or churches, schools, and libraries. A crude textbook was prepared by staff members and mimeographed for use in the early classes. This delay in delivery of supplies in turn meant delay in teaching since it was necessary to gather the materials, write the textbook and reproduce it before starting instruction. Space was also a problem for the program. It was not until about the 15th of July that space for the administrative offices and two classrooms was provided in the old furniture store and warehouse taken over by PUL at 47 West 125th Street. Locating space for the reading centers was also difficult, and these were not set up until about the fourth week of the program. All of these problems perhaps contributed to one serious weakness in the remedial reading program, the lack of tests and reading level scores which could have identified any improvement in reading level over the course of the summer. There is no question that a good deal of reading instruction occurred during the summer and undoubtedly there was some improvement. Because the effort is so clearly evident, it is particularly unfortunate that no figures were available on what the reading program really accomplished. Without these before and after reading scores, it is impossible to judge the effectiveness of the program except to commend the staff and enrollees for overcoming numerous obstacles in organization.

Vest-Pocket Parks

The objective of the vest-pocket park program was to construct small parks on ten vacant lot sites throughout Harlem. The construction of these parks would then provide "improved facilities for the general use of residents in the area," "an increase in residential participation in local organizations," "an enhanced self-concept for the enrollees working in the program," and "instructions for enrollees in how to handle construction tools, materials, and elementary work skills." Some 163 enrollees and twenty-three supervisors were employed in the vest-pocket park program under the direction of the Harlem Neighborhood Association. By the end of the summer project in September three parks had been completed. Two more that were awaiting black-topping (the final work stage), and one that had been leveled, were completed in the fall after the end of Project Uplift.

In looking at the problems of all the work programs, the delay in delivery of supplies has been a constant theme. In the vest-pocket park program these delays were particularly disastrous since it was impossible to improvise or find substitutes for shovels, pick axes, dump trucks, and other heavy equipment required for the construction of these parks. In the early weeks of the summer project there was virtually nothing for some of the work crews to do. Each step of the construction procedure had to be done in proper sequence. Thus if a bulldozer scheduled for a particular day did not arrive, work on the vest-pocket park stopped. An additional problem was the lack of skill and experience of a number of supervisors. Trained workers were needed for leveling and building retaining walls in the parks. The payroll problem which affected all parts of PUL was also evident here. Friday, August 20th, was the first week in which all enrollees in the vest-pocket park program were paid on time.

The park sites were not scattered throughout central Harlem, but in fact were clustered quite close together. Three sites were within a block or two of Mt. Morris Park and three others close to Millbank Center, a large, already existing recreation center. No reason can be found for these locations and in fact the responsibility for selecting them could not be placed. Another fundamental question which must be asked about this particular program is why it was assigned to the Harlem Neighborhood Association. HANA as an organization had no previous experience with a park building program and indeed during PUL's planning stage requested a recreation program. It was informed that ACT has been assigned the recreation component and HANA was then offered the vest-pocket park program. Two errors seem to have been made here: 1) on the part of HARYOU planners in offering this specialized and rather technical construction program to an organization with no experience in this field, and 2) a mistake on the part of HANA in accepting an assignment which lay outside of its own experience.

Information Booths

The objective of this program was to set up information booths in the major shopping areas of central Harlem. These booths manned by PUL enrollees were planned to provide a wide variety of information about New York City and the social services available to residents of Harlem. The rationale for this program was that "poor and under-educated people were frequently reluctant to visit offices with facilities which appear formal in any way." These booths would then be able to dispense information and direction for people reluctant to enter an office. By August 20th, five information booths had been constructed. In addition a seventy-page directory was compiled by the staff and enrollees which contained brief information on New York City resources on health, housing, welfare, community organizations, religious organizations, and educational facilities.

Clearly the major problem connected with the information booth program was the delay in construction. The report for the week of August 9th, the sixth week of the program, indicated that only one booth was in operation. It was not until the end of the eighth week that all five booths were operating. The Urban League's building repair program had the responsibility for constructing the booths. The delay in receiving building materials and tools was evident in this program as in all others. It was originally planned that records of requests for information and other inquiries would be kept as an aid in evaluating the program, as well as for determining the needs of local residents. This was not done. As a result there is no way of telling how many requests were made, or what questions were asked of the enrollees manning the booths. Three supervisors and twenty-six enrollees were involved in this project, but because of the delay in building the booths, most of these enrollees were assigned temporarily to other work programs. The constructing and manning of information booths in Harlem seem to have been a good idea and as outlined in the original proposal would have served a useful function in the Harlem community. Because of the extended delay in beginning this program and the complete lack of any record keeping, this work program must be judged to have been a good idea which was almost a complete failure in operation.

Historical Landmarks

This program vehicle was also under the supervision of the Harlem Administrative Committee. Its objective was to identify sites of historical events in Harlem and the birthplaces and residences of persons who have made significant contributions to American life. Historical markers were then to be painted and posted on these sites. PUL enrollees would be trained to conduct guided tours of these landmarks, providing information about the history of Harlem, for children in the day camps.

Unfortunately the historical landmarks must be classified along with the information booths as a good idea which was not carried out effectively during the summer. There is no doubt that in the early weeks difficulties relating to supplies affected this program as well as all the rest. But there was no evidence that any historical markers were placed on Harlem buildings and although several tours were conducted for day-camp youngsters there is no information available on how many tours or how many youngsters were involved. Only half a dozen enrollees were in the program along with one supervisor who was an historian. The reasons for the failure of this program other than the supply difficulty remain obscure. Although research was done and sites were identified, the educational and community service part of this program did not develop.

Emergency Homemaker Service

The objectives of the emergency homemaker service as described in the proposal for Project Uplift were to recruit, train, and employ young women (PUL enrollees) to serve as emergency homemakers for families in critical situations. This service was to provide instruction in child care, home management, family finance and would be used as a basis for creating positive attitudes in these young women toward family life. The service was to be made available to Harlem residents through local social agencies. Forty-two PUL enrollees and two supervisors were employed in this program. During the ten week life of PUL only eleven cases of service were provided to families in central Harlem. Each case involved an average of four visits to each family, each visit lasting approximately five hours. The enrollees performed a variety of tasks, including general cleaning, preparation of foods, and child care. The housewives who received the service were favorably impressed and indicated that they would like to see the program continued on a year-round basis. It is apparent from the above figures that forty-two enrollees were not kept busy in this program. Many were temporarily assigned to day camps and recreation programs.

The most serious problem connected with the emergency homemaker service seems to have been the inability of this program to make itself widely known in the Harlem community. Attempts were made to find families who needed this service through local churches and other community organizations. As might be expected the requests for this service began to come to the homemaker supervisors toward the end of the summer. Had this program been continued it would have had more requests than it could have handled. It was unreasonable for the project planners to expect a program of this nature, dependent in good part on requests for service coming to the supervisors, to become fully operative in a matter of a few days. An emergency homemaker service seems much more appropriate for a year-round project rather than one of only ten weeks.

Another related problem which would certainly face an extended family service program was that of communicable disease. Should enrollees enter a home where there was sickness without a doctor's assurance that there was no communicable disease present? If the service was designed to be for crisis situations it would seem impossible to receive this medical assurance in time to be of use in the crisis. There was no evidence from the emergency homemaker service program that the limited experience in family service had any impact on the enrollees' attitudes toward family life. In a more extended program it might well be possible to discover whether this service experience would in fact affect young women's attitudes toward family responsibility.

Tree Planting

The objective of this program was to plant 1500 trees in central Harlem. Enrollees were to be responsible for preparing the sites and doing the actual planting under professional supervision. The responsibility for maintaining the trees after the summer would be passed on to selected local agencies. The tree planting failed totally in reaching its objective during the ten weeks of PUL's life. By the middle of September only one tree had been planted. The enrollees and supervisors originally assigned to this project were transferred to the building repairs program.

It was discovered that, first of all, trees should not be transplanted during the summer months. Consequently the New York City Commissioner of Parks refused to give permits for planting trees on public property. It was also discovered after the beginning of the project that city-approved nurseries charged approximately three times as much per tree as suburban nurseries with whom arrangements had already been made The estimated cost of the program had, of course, been based on the lower figure. A compromise was eventually reached when the Commissioner of Parks agreed to allow the planting of trees from suburban nurseries after October 1st. Selected tree planting crews were formed and by the end of November 371 trees had been planted in central Harlem. It is certainly clear from the problems mentioned above that a tree-planting program has no place in a summer project. In a year-round project, however, the planting of trees when coordinated with building repairs, painting, etc. could certainly contribute to a more attractive community.

Neighborhood Development

The objectives stated for the neighborhood development program included: 1) the assignment of workers (PUL enrollees) to help organize and staff block associations; 2) an evaluation of each participating block and neighborhood organization to be undertaken at the beginning of the summer; and 3) attendance of consultants and enrollees at meetings of local organizations to act as resource persons. This program vehicle seems to have been completely overlooked in the operation of PUL. There is no evidence that any work was done with block associations, that any survey was taken, or that any consultation was provided to local organizations in Harlem. The administrative responsibility for this program was with the central staff of PUL, and apparently there were simply no personnel available to administer and staff such a program. It is unfortunate that in a project such as Project Uplift, designed in part to offer services to the larger community, this particular program was not implemented. HARYOU had been engaged prior to the summer in a similar program, but certainly the additional field staff and professional consultants called for in PUL's proposal would have been useful.

Youth Congress

Plans for a Youth Congress to be directed and planned by PUL enrollees were first conceived about August 1st. During the first week of August the Public Relations Department brought together about twenty enrollees representing most of the work programs and administrative departments. This initial meeting was to plan for a Youth Congress in which the enrollees would be free to discuss the strengths and weaknesses of the entire summer project and make recommendations for changes. At this initial meeting there was criticism expressed. "Headquarters is not doing its job." "There are too many supervisors running around." "The ideas of the program are fine but they are not being carried out."

It was clear from this initial meeting that the representatives did want a Youth Congress and specifically one in which they would be free to express themselves fully and frankly. They suggested attendance by representatives from all PUL activities and departments. They also wanted to include the press, the mayor or a representative from his office, and a representative from the Office of Economic Opportunity. The enrollees clearly wanted to run their own show and believed they were acting within the guidelines of the OEO, i.e., encouraging those who are affected by poverty programs to have a voice in their operations. These proposals were put in writing and submitted to the PUL administration.

They were modified to some extent in that no outside guests, press or governmental, were to be invited; and, it was urged that the enrollees would concentrate on a constructive evaluation of the various stages of PUL's program. The Youth Congress was held in the third week of August and was attended by only twenty-five enrollees representing less than half of the programs in PUL. Also present were ten youth workers, members of HARYOU's permanent staff. A clear conflict was apparent early in the morning session of the Congress since PUL enrollees wanted to discuss the merits and shortcomings of their programs, while the HARYOU youth workers wanted to discuss the relationship between PUL and HARYOU. The general feeling of the HARYOU youth workers was that "PUL was a waste and a duplication of already existing HARYOU activity." The administration of PUL also came in for criticism with one HARYOU worker asking, "Why did they hire specialists and consultants? They can all go downtown and get a job. Let's have fewer outsiders and more local people." Another important grievance voiced by the HARYOU employees was the higher pay given to many PUL enrollees (the associate category, age 21-25, received $80 per week). This conflict between the youth workers of HARYOU and the PUL enrollees was indicative of points of conflict between the whole of Project Uplift and its parent organization. It is probably true that the opinions and attitudes expressed by the young people employed by HARYOU were representative of opinion at higher levels. Some of this resentment is inevitable when additional personnel are taken on for a short period of time. It is particularly likely when the special project is larger at all levels than the parent organization. The conflict between local people and outside experts is an extremely important and fundamental one. It is a dilemma which continues to plague all poverty programs, the conflict between two important values, the training and employing of people from the community affected by the program over against the effective and efficient operation of the program to its stated goals.

In the afternoon session of the Youth Congress a motion was passed calling for a panel discussion between representatives of the enrollees and the various department heads of Project Uplift. This meeting was held two weeks later on September 2nd. The enrollees asked a great variety of questions about problems such as supplies and payroll. Although they were probably not completely satisfied by the answers, they at least had the satisfaction of hearing the department heads and project coordinator attempt to answer them in person.

Special Community Related Programs

The following programs have been described in some detail in the preceding chapter "Project Uplift and the Harlem Community." It seems appropriate here, however, to mention them in terms of their particular strengths and weaknesses and their contributions to Project Uplift as a whole.

Community Survey Section

The community survey section administratively placed under the Community and Public Relations Department was one of the twelve work programs. Its primary purpose was to survey the Harlem community on a number of issues and in addition to inform people interviewed about the project. As spelled out in Chapter VI the main problem with this program was that the results of its surveys could not be used to make statements about the Harlem community as a whole since proper sampling and research procedures were not used. This was unfortunate since there was evidence of considerable hard work and high motivation on the part of enrollees.

Black Arts Repertory Theatre

The Black Arts Repertory Theatre was a special program which did not appear in the original proposal but was added midway in the summer. The level of dramatic and artistic activity in this program seemed to be high. The main problem from PUL's point of view, however, was the ideology of LeRoi Jones, the director of the theater, and the subject matter and ideological position expressed in the dramatic presentations. Although there was no other theater group in Harlem which could have developed a training program for enrollees in the time required, some of the unfavorable comments in the general press should have been anticipated by those who drew up and approved this special program.

Harlem Olympics

The Harlem Olympics, another special project, directed by the recreation program of the Associated Community Teams, was quite successful. It involved five different district competitions as well as the final "Olympics" held on August 28th at Randalls Island Stadium. The only disappointing aspect of this program was the failure of the participants' parents and the general Harlem public to attend the event. From the point of view of the contestants it was clearly one of the most popular and talked about activities during the course of the summer.

Final Parade and Festival

The final parade and festival must also be considered as a special project. Although the parade included representatives of other HARYOU programs in addition to Project Uplift, the organization, planning and operation of this day were entirely the responsibility of PUL's Community and Public Relations Department. For the PUL enrollees this special final day seemed to end the summer project on a note of success and pride in accomplishment.

Major Weaknesses of Project Uplift

Lack of Lead Time

Many of the operational problems encountered during the ten-week life of Project Uplift can be traced to a fundamental weakness which was the lack of lead time both for planning and phasing into full operation. As stated earlier the project was conceived late in the spring of 1965 and hurriedly put together. The first proposal submitted to the Office of Economic Opportunity was turned down with the suggestion that it be rewritten to qualify as a demonstration project under Section 207 of the Economic Opportunity Act of 1964. This meant complete rewriting and restructuring of many work programs with the starting date, June 28, only weeks away. It seems likely that if the creators of Project Uplift had begun their planning in December, 1964, or January, 1965, many of the bugs which were discovered in the proposal only when it was already in operation might well have been caught in an earlier draft.

This extended planning period would certainly have resulted in a smoother and more effective operation. For example, if more time had been available it seems likely that one of the planners would have discovered the inappropriateness of planting 1500 trees in the summer. Feelers could have been put out to the Park Commissioner before the start of the summer project and the tree planting component could have been quietly shelved. More planning time would have allowed for consultation with a larger number of community leaders in Harlem, as well as experts in many fields. Because of the pressures of time this kind of consultation was almost nonexistent. The second problem which grew out of the lack of planning time was that no allowance was made for phasing into full operation. In retrospect it seems totally inexcusable that the money for Project Uplift was not finally approved until June 25th, three days before the starting date of June 28th. In the proposal there were included a number of initial steps to be taken prior to the start of the program on June 28th. Many of these steps, such as obtaining information about staff facilities of local organizations which were to participate in the program and canvassing block associations for their needs, were never carried out. The preliminary training program for both staff and enrollees contained in the original proposal was severely curtailed and, in fact, most training was done by the local organizations on-the-job. HARYOU assigned several staff members to PUL for the initial planning phase. But the four contracting organizations, Associated Community Teams, HANA, HAC, and the Urban League of Greater New York were all either unwilling or unable to make personnel available before funds were actually released by the government. This reluctance on their part was understandable since there have been projects and plans which have fallen through at the last minute and all of these organizations had other on-going programs. The result was, of course, that the work program in all phases was inevitably behind schedule. For example, by July 19th in the fourth week of the program, no contracts had yet been signed with the four prime contracting agencies mentioned above. With all of the inevitable problems associated with mounting a short-term, large scale project, it was extremely unfortunate that more time could not have been provided for both planning and phasing in.

Delays in Purchasing and Distributing Supplies and Equipment

One of the most serious and wide-spread problems which faced all the work programs in Project Uplift in the early weeks was the failure to receive urgently needed supplies and equipment. To understand the reason for this it is necessary to look at the provisions made for obtaining and distributing supplies and the methods used to achieve this end. The original proposal contained no special reference to a supply department or any section that could be interpreted as fulfilling that function; so the office of supply expediter was created at the suggestion of the Office of Economic Opportunity. The purpose of this department was to facilitate and speed up the requisitioning, purchasing and distributing of all furnishings, equipment, and supplies to the central staff, the contracting agencies, and the subcontracting agencies or local organizations. It must be clear in the reader's mind that this office had no direct or indirect authority to initiate requests or authorize purchases for any supplies or materials. The requests initiated logically enough with the various departments and local agencies and were authorized by the comptroller's office of HARYOU. No separate authority for purchasing supplies, paying bills or salaries was established.

Provisions in the original proposal called for the addition of several personnel to the comptroller's office but these proved to be totally inadequate. PUL, after all, was spending more money for supplies, equipment, and salaries in ten weeks than HARYOU would spend in a calendar year. It is surprising that the comptroller of HARYOU did not realize that the addition of several bookkeepers and an assistant comptroller would be inadequate. The initial plan was for all supply requests to flow through the PUL supply expediter where they were to be analyzed in regard to budget lines and assembled for purchase in bulk lots. This procedure quickly broke down. Purchase requests were taken directly to the comptroller's office or purchases were made by individuals and agencies without coordination with either the comptroller's office or the supply expediter's office. With more lead time available the extent of the supply problem might have been reduced, but since no purchases could be authorized before June 25 and the program was supposed to be fully operative on June 28, the massive number of supply requests in this initial period simply could not be processed, purchased, and distributed in three days. If the money could have been made available two weeks before the start of the project and if departments and agencies could have submitted their requests at that time, and if an adequate staff could have been added to the comptroller's office, it seems likely that supply would not have been the major problem that it was.

An alternative administrative arrangement would have been to set up a completely separate comptroller's office for Project Uplift. This was done, for example, in such areas as personnel, legal affairs, public relations, and program development and training. There might well have been an objection to this idea from leaders of HARYOU since this would have meant virtual independence for PUL.

Delays and Inaccuracies in the Payroll

Closely related to the delay in receiving supplies were the delays and inaccuracies in payments to supervisors and enrollees in PUL. The payroll procedures were generally as follows: time cards for each enrollee and staff member signed by a supervisor or department head were to be submitted to the payroll office on Monday for the previous week with checks being issued the following Friday. This procedure broke down in several ways. Some organizations were late in turning in their cards thus not giving the payroll department enough time to process the checks. In other cases time cards were submitted with no signature or an incorrect signature, resulting in their not being honored by the payroll department. To add to the problem there was simply not an adequate staff to handle the volume of payroll in the comptroller's office. By the middle of the summer project over 4000 checks were being issued each week.

The effect of delays and inaccuracies is extremely hard to measure but it was certainly a serious one. On a questionnaire administered to enrollees at the end of the project, 40 per cent indicated that late or inaccurate payment was the thing they disliked most about their summer job. On another question over two-thirds identified "I was not paid on time" or "I was not paid the correct amount" as being true about their job during the summer. If all these administrative problems had not existed, it would have aided considerably the evaluation of the project since enrollees and supervisors would in these questions have been forced to comment on more basic aspects of the program. Over 70 per cent of the supervisors, too, indicated that enrollees not being paid on time made their job as supervisors more difficult. The magnitude of the problem was, of course, not unknown to the administrators of PUL. Beginning on July 12 a special payroll department was established to process and verify the time cards prior to their being handed on to the comptroller's office. The creation of this department tended to decrease the magnitude of this problem in the latter weeks of the summer, although it was never completely solved. The project planners again failed to take into consideration the vast number of checks that had to be issued and the staff members needed to do the job.

Relations with HARYOU

In several different places in the description and analysis of Project Uplift, its relationship to HARYOU has been mentioned. Clearly, some of the problems between the board of directors and staff of HARYOU, and the staff of Project Uplift would be inevitable. PUL was a lavishly financed, short-term, large-scale summer project which was nominally a project of HARYOU. Yet in fact the great majority of staff members on all levels had not previously and would not at the end of the summer be HARYOU employees. Another complicating factor was that where comparable departments were set up such as public relations, personnel, legal affairs and training, it was sometimes true that the department head in PUL had better qualifications for the position than his or her opposite number in HARYOU. Thus personal concern for job security and in some cases jealousy entered the picture. It was also true, although not on the highest level, that some Project Uplift employees were paid higher salaries than HARYOU employees for equivalent work, particularly in the associate category (21-25) of the enrollees who received $80 per week.

There was some evidence as the summer progressed that top leaders and board members of HARYOU were becoming concerned with the publicity and press notices given to Project Uplift. They felt that the sponsorship of HARYOU was not made clear in this publicity and also felt with some justification, that their own summer projects were completely overshadowed by Project Uplift. The weeks of wrangling over who would sponsor and participate in the Final Parade and Festival Day were a result of this concern on the part of HARYOU leaders. There was perhaps a personal element in this concern as well since neither these top leaders nor their regular staff were directly involved in PUL programs. One or two indicated during the summer that they felt PUL had turned into a "frankenstein" monster. Another said that Project Uplift has really "put us in the shade this summer, even in Harlem." For the course of the summer of 1965 it was to some extent true that the tail was wagging the dog.

In view of these strong feelings and attitudes toward PUL, it would seem that future planners of similar projects in the poverty field should consider carefully the relationship between a massive, short-term project and the on-going agency under which it is subsumed. It would seem appropriate either to: 1) make sure that an agency funded for a special project can handle it reasonably well within its own structure or with the addition of a few personnel or, 2) consider separate funding to a special agency set up for the particular purpose of the short-term project, and which could be dismantled completely when the project was terminated. It might be the case that community organizations like HARYOU would object to establishing an independent structure in Harlem for such a project, and even that a separate structure would be in violation of the "war on poverty" principle of involving local community individuals and groups in programs which affect them. But for a project of the magnitude and complexity of PUL, and in a community where no organization exists which could easily or adequately incorporate such a project within its own structure, it would seem reasonable at least to consider separate funding. This separate funding need not mean that residents of the community or local organizations would not participate. But only that independent fiscal and legal responsibility would be established.

Relations with Local Agencies

Closely related to the problem of Project Uplift vis-a-vis HARYOU was the problem of PUL vis-a-vis the four contracting agencies (HAC, HANA, ACT, and the Urban League), and local organizations. The main problem here was one of ill-defined lines of responsibility and accountability. To whom was a day camp operated by a neighborhood church really responsible? ACT was the contracting agency with responsibility for day-camp programs. But supplies were requested (in some cases) from the supply expediter's office of PUL. They were approved and purchased, however, by the comptroller of HARYOU. Advice and "assistance" came also from several sources. ACT had its own supervisory staff who were, so they believed, responsible for the programs developed by all day camps. The program development and training department of Project Uplift was charged with the mission of assisting in program development and training of enrollees assigned to all phases of the program. Representatives of this department would also visit day-camp sites offering advice and in some cases giving orders. HARYOU, fiscally responsible for the program to the federal government, was of course also concerned with activities in all phases of the project; so investigators and inspectors would visit day-camp sites from the central office of HARYOU as well. All of this as might be expected led to considerable confusion and some bad feeling on the part of local organization leaders. This problem in part may be traced back to the nature of Project Uplift's relationship with HARYOU, but even within the terms established it would have been possible to make very clear the lines of authority and responsibility. The evaluation department of PUL, which also had to make on-site inspections and conduct interviews, attempted to alleviate this problem by checking in with the contracting agency before visiting local work sites. This allowed ACT, for example, to let a day camp know that it was to be visited by a representative of the evaluation office.

*The Lack of an Adequate Job Development
and Guidance Program*

One question that was on the minds of all enrollees was, what happens to me when the summer is over? No provision was made in PUL's original proposal for dealing with this question. On the initiative of the project coordinator in the sixth week of the project the job development and guidance department was established. The objectives of this department included assisting enrollees either to return to high school or for those who were qualified to enter or continue their education on the college level; discovering as many full and part-time jobs as possible for enrollees; referring enrollees to other social agencies with job placement units; and securing scholarship assistance for prospective college students with financial need.

Starting in the sixth week of the program greatly reduced the amount of work this department could accomplish. It did manage to obtain about eighty college scholarships for enrollees at various colleges throughout the country and to locate over 600 part-time and over 200 full-time jobs. With a staff of fifty-five enrollees and a dozen supervisors working for only five weeks, this seems to be about all that could reasonably be expected. In terms of the total number of enrollees in PUL (approximately 4000) the number served by the job development and guidance department was not large. It seems an incredible oversight that such an important service, especially for a short-term summer project, was not planned as an integral part of the original proposal. It may have been assumed that enrollees in PUL would make use of HARYOU's job placement and guidance office. But here again, HARYOU was not equipped to deal with the numbers involved. Had a PUL job development and guidance office been set up at the beginning of the project, it is certain that the long range value of PUL would have been considerably increased.

The Value of Short-Term Projects

The above discussion of a job development and guidance department leads naturally into the somewhat broader question about the inherent value of any short-term project. It is no secret that the chief motivation for many of those who pushed for the idea of a summer project was to "cool it" in Harlem during the summer, in other words keep Harlem's young people off the street and out of trouble. This is not to say that for those involved in the program this was the only or even the most important purpose. But it was clearly in the minds of those who were pushing for such a program in the spring. With this original motivation it is perhaps remarkable that things went as well as they did during the summer. This concern for "cooling it" certainly contributed to the lack of attention paid to the problem of providing long range benefit to those who participated in the program. No suggestions were made for connecting PUL to any of the year-round activities of HARYOU or other agencies in the Harlem community. In the time available for planning the project, extensive thought about this problem was impossible. But if a short-term project is to have any real effect on those participating, its relationship with longer range training programs, employment services, and educational institutions must be carefully designed and implemented.

Demonstration Project

The decision made by OEO late in the spring to turn PUL into a demonstration project requires some comment at this point. A demonstration project should test certain hypotheses and program vehicles and try to show which hypotheses and vehicles were successful and should be replicated in future programs. It was unfortunate that a number of the original hypotheses were not testable as the project developed. Certainly some of the hypotheses themselves were ill conceived. A more important criticism, however, of the "demonstration" aspect of PUL must be made with reference to the complete lack of provision for follow-up studies. A number of hypotheses were stated relating to changes which might occur in the self-image of Harlem youth involved in the project. Others related to the strengthening of local organizations, while still others referred to improved educational performance of Harlem youth, especially in reading. To test adequately any of these hypotheses it would be necessary to interview and question PUL enrollees and local organization leaders at least one year after the end of the summer project. It would also be necessary to examine school records and interview the teachers of PUL enrollees. No financial provision was made for this follow-up research in the original proposal nor at this writing has there been any additional research program initiated by the federal government. Since nothing is known about the project's long range effect on Harlem's young people or its local organizations, it is extremely doubtful that Project Uplift in a scientific sense demonstrates anything. The responsibility for this oversight must be assigned to federal anti-poverty officials, since both leaders of PUL and HARYOU urged that such follow-up evaluation be planned while the project was in operation.

Strengths of Project Uplift

The reader at this point may be tempted to think of PUL as an almost completely wasted effort which failed to accomplish its stated purposes. In spite of the criticisms contained in the preceding section, Project Uplift was by no means a total failure. As is usually the case, it is easier to be specific and precise about weaknesses than it is about strengths. Nevertheless there are several ways in which PUL can be judged to have been successful.

1.) It is important to remember that the project was conceived as a special summer employment program for Harlem youth between the ages of fourteen and twenty-five. The original proposal called for employing 2500 youth for a period of ten weeks. In fact by the sixth week of the program, 4000 Harlem youth were employed in various work activities. In other words considering the lack of planning time and the lack of foresight in realizing certain personnel needs in terms of payroll and supply, the fact that PUL developed an on-going program on any level of functioning must be judged to be in itself a considerable accomplishment. In spite of inaccuracies and delays in the payroll it is a fact that all PUL enrollees received monies due them. Although there is no evidence concerning just how all the enrollees spent their money, there are numerous individual examples of enrollees being able to continue their education using the income derived from PUL. It is an understatement to say that summer jobs are difficult for young black men and women to find, particularly those who have not completed high school. PUL, then, did at least provide them with employment at a salary which enabled many of them to save some portion of their earnings.

2.) A number of the work programs in PUL must be judged as reasonably successful in achieving and in some cases exceeding their original goals. Leading these would be the day camp, residential camp, and athletic workshop programs administered by ACT and the building repair program administered by the Urban League. In spite of the payroll and supply problems spelled out in the preceding section these two programs organized themselves quickly and for the most part used enrollees assigned to them in useful and even creative ways. Public relations, although not designated as a work program in the original proposal, performed its functions well by training a selected number of enrollees in communications skills, and by informing both the Project Uplift personnel and the general public about the summer's activities. Those special projects organized with the public in mind, such as the Harlem Olympics and the Parade and Festival Day were exceptionally well done.

3.) In two important and related ways, the attitudes of the enrollees were affected favorably by their summer experience. At the end of the summer when asked the question, "If you had your choice, would you like most to live in a neighborhood which is 'all Negro,' 'mostly Negro,' 'mixed Negro and white,' 'mostly white' or 'all white'?", significantly more selected "all Negro" or "mostly Negro" than they had at the beginning of the summer. This can reasonably be interpreted as an increase in the racial identification of the enrollees. Perhaps an even more important indication of value in the program is the fact that more enrollees were optimistic about the prospect of improving conditions in Harlem at the end of the summer than at the beginning. At the summer's end, 70 per cent judged the prospects to be "very good" or "good." This optimism, although perhaps based on some unrealistic assumptions about existing problems, is surely a necessary ingredient for producing any significant change in a slum community like Harlem.

4.) An important additional strength of PUL was the fact that almost all of the staff who organized and directed the project were from central Harlem and that where it was necessary to obtain special talents from outside the community, a real attempt was made to employ black consultants. This use of local and especially black professional staff provided important role models for the enrollees in the project. Too frequently in the past, projects designed to "help the community" have been planned, directed and operated by outside professionals who were, more likely than not, white. It was not true that Project Uplift was an entirely black project since whites occupied positions ranging from department heads down to enrollees. The important thing is that blacks and local Harlem residents predominated in positions of authority and in all cases (since the project coordinator as well as the executive director of HARYOU were black) white staff members were responsible to and took orders from blacks. It may well be that some of the increased identification with the Harlem community grew out of observing this kind of black-white relationship on all levels of the project. A small minority of staff and enrollees could be identified as "black nationalist." They, of course, questioned the presence of any white workers on any level of the project. Despite these feelings the working relationships between black and white staff members were good. There was no evidence of any overt racial conflict occurring during the life of PUL. The idea of black leadership and black responsibility for community projects in Harlem was not original with Project Uplift but in fact was taken over from the philosophy of its parent organization, HARYOU.

5.) Another vital aspect of PUL, although difficult to measure, was the value of the experience provided for staff and some enrollees in performing supervisory and administrative tasks for which they had no previous training. There is no question that PUL employed at all levels below department heads, professional staff and enrollees in positions for which they were not qualified by educational background or in some cases experience. The stated philosophy of the "war on poverty" was that wherever possible local residents should be employed even in cases where they were not fully qualified in the normal employment-office sense of that word. Now clearly this policy had to result in problems related to over-all efficiency and smoothness of operation. There is a further difficulty with the definition of terms. "Not fully qualified" is one thing while "totally unqualified" is something else. In spite of these difficulties PUL provided a vast training ground for young black men and women who had never before had the opportunity of assuming responsibility for supervising and directing programs in their community.

Summary: What Can Be Learned From Project Uplift?

1) PUL was called in the newspaper accounts a "crash program." Someone has described a crash program as "when you get nine women pregnant and then hope to have a baby in one month." The point is that for certain things including babies and complicated massive work programs for young people, a certain period of time is absolutely necessary. The project gestation period was far too short and as has already been pointed out many other problems stem from this fact. The word "crash" has other and unfortunate connotations, and it would be well if all agencies permanently removed the word from their operational vocabulary.

2) Extreme care must be taken in planning the mechanics of a program like PUL. More care in working out the procedures for ordering supplies and for paying staff and enrollees would have reduced the problems of the project greatly over the course of the summer. Both supply and payroll are rather low-level and routine functions. They are not the exciting aspects of the proposal and their smooth functioning will not get anybody much public credit. Their failure to function in Project Uplift, however, caused virtually all of the unfavorable accounts which appeared in the press. The effects on the morale of the enrollees and staff were hard to measure but were certainly present. Sufficient personnel must be planned for and assigned to these routine but crucially important tasks.

3) A short-term summer project to maximize its effectiveness should, wherever possible, support or supplement already existing programs in the community. The day-camp and athletic workshop programs did this to a higher degree than any other work program. They did not attempt to compete with or set up only new day camps. But, rather, they enabled many local organizations to expand their programs with the help of PUL money, supplies, and added staff in the form of enrollees. Some new day camps were established and these were strengthened by being related through PUL to local organizations which had considerable experience in this area. Those parts of Project Uplift which did not attempt to relate their work to any other programs in the Harlem community fared less well. The homemaker program, for example, which attempted to provide services

somewhat like those already being provided by professional social welfare agencies in Harlem, never really succeeded. Its failure was perhaps in part due to this lack of coordination with already existing programs.

4) In planning a massive short-term project considerable care must be given to this project's relationship with already existing community organizations and social agencies. HARYOU was clearly not equipped in terms of staff to take on Project Uplift. It was necessary to hire virtually the entire staff from outside HARYOU. As has been pointed out earlier this caused some difficulty in the relationship between PUL and HARYOU. The fact that "outsiders" were for the most part directing PUL, clearly reduced the feeling of responsibility which the HARYOU staff felt for Project Uplift's success or failure. This psychological condition was certainly not a desirable one for the success of the project. Given the lack of planning time between conception and the proposed execution perhaps no other arrangement was possible. But it would certainly be important for federal agencies considering similar projects in the future to keep this relationship in mind.

5) Short-term projects should be planned whenever possible to feed into long range education, training, and employment programs. In Harlem there exists a considerable number of permanent social agencies which would have been able to assist PUL enrollees in many ways. However, in the original Project Uplift proposal no provision was made for directing and guiding the enrollees to these other agencies. In particular a summer employment program should attempt to direct its workers to those who could find permanent employment based on the summer experience or to those agencies which would encourage and assist youngsters to continue their education. A belated attempt was made by the creation of the job training and development department but it was unable to do the job. This lack of tie-in was also unfortunate for the professional and secretarial staff of the summer project, many of whom were unable to obtain employment at the end of the summer.

6) For any federal poverty program funded under the demonstration title, follow-up evaluation is crucially important. To make sound judgments about the effects of PUL on those

involved it is essential to know what, if any, effect the project had on their lives one or two years after the experience. Admittedly this evaluation is difficult to obtain and expensive, but if the purpose of a demonstration project is in fact to demonstrate whether or not one or another program and technique was effective, it is essential that the federal government make available to program planners at all levels the kind of information which can only be secured through follow-up evaluation.

7) Careful consideration should be given to the relative merits of funding a short-term, crash program like PUL as opposed to using this money to support longer range programs pursuing the same goals and objectives. We have already discussed the motivation for funding PUL. "Cooling" Harlem for the summer necessitated a summer project. But if this motivation is rejected as it should be, then the merits of short-term vs. long range must be considered. It is not suggested here that short-term programs should not exist, but rather that the government make a careful analysis of the existing problems, the existing programs designed to deal with them, and the most effective use of federal money.

8) In all poverty programs, wherever possible, local community residents should be employed and employed on levels for which they might not be fully qualified. This statement reflects a central theme of the philosophy of the "war on poverty" which is that people affected by a program should be involved in its planning and execution. At the same time neither the government nor the public can expect a smooth and completely professional operation. There will be problems because of a lack of skill and unfamiliarity with assigned tasks. In a longer range program these difficulties should become less severe over time. During PUL's ten weeks, this development was clearly present. Even the supply and payroll problem decreased in importance as the summer progressed. It is true that in certain key positions professional leadership will be needed and in some cases this leadership must be recruited from outside the community. This should be done, however, only when it is absolutely necessary.

9) The federal government and the public should have realistic expectations for a short-term project such as PUL. In the

original proposal it was hypothesized that the young people involved in the program would be affected in a variety of ways,
many of them representing fundamental changes in their attitudes toward life, toward themselves, and toward the Harlem
community. It is now apparent that these expectations were
quite unrealistic. A ten- or eleven-week work program is simply
too short a time and not an intensive enough experience to
change fundamentally either attitudes or the community itself.
This does not mean that short-term projects can accomplish
nothing. In two areas, racial identification and optimism about
solving problems in Harlem, the summer experience did produce
a modest change in the attitude of PUL enrollees. A sure way to
produce failure in the eyes of both politicians and the public at
large is to begin with expectations that cannot reasonably be
achieved. This lesson is particularly applicable to short-term
projects. Fundamental change will come only through long and
intensive efforts, not through summer crash programs.

10) In all poverty programs, whether short-range or long-
term, every effort must be made to relate what is done to the
basic problems of the community served. The Harlem community leaders interviewed during the course of Project Uplift,
again and again pointed to this as a fundamental criticism. They
identified at least two problems, that of the lack of permanent
employment opportunities and the lack of educational opportunities as being basic for the Harlem community. PUL did not
and was not designed to make an impact in these areas. For
example, although several reading centers happened to be
located in public schools and although some teachers in Harlem
schools were employed during the summer, no systematic attempt was made to utilize the educational facilities available in
Harlem. Project Uplift left the Harlem community certainly no
worse but perhaps in any fundamental sense little better than
before the summer began.

CHAPTER EIGHT

Community Control
and the Future of Poverty

A recipe for violence: Promise a lot; deliver a little. Lead people to believe they will be much better off, but let there be no dramatic improvement. Try a variety of small programs, each interesting but marginal in impact and severely underfinanced. Avoid any attempted solution remotely comparable in size to the dimensions of the problem you are trying to solve. Have middle-class civil servants hire upper-class student radicals to use lower-class Negroes as a battering ram against the existing local political systems; then complain that people are going around disrupting things and chastise local politicians for not cooperating with those out to do them in. Get some poor people involved in local decision-making, only to discover that there is not enough at stake to be worth bothering about. Feel guilty about what has happened to black people; tell them you are surprised they have not revolted before; express shock and dismay when they follow your advice. Go in for a little force, just enough to anger, not enough to discourage. Feel guilty again; say you are surprised that worse has not happened. Alternate with a little suppression. Mix well, apply a match, and run ....[1]

This quotation describes in rather dramatic form what has happened to the "war on poverty" since the summer of 1965. Indeed the violence predicted began that summer with Watts. Riots, disturbances, and uprisings have come to characterize summers in urban slums across the United States. Although most widespread and destructive in the summer of 1967, violence in black slums has broken out each summer since 1965.

[1] Aaron Wildavsky, as quoted in Daniel P. Moynihan, *Maximum Feasible Misunderstanding* (New York: Free Press, 1969).

An important associated development over the past five years has been what can only be described as the gradual death of the "war on poverty." For at least the last two years one searches liberal journals in vain for the use of this phrase or the underlying assumptions that the Office of Economic Opportunity or federally financed and directed programs should continue to play any significant part in the attempt to reduce and eliminate poverty in the United States. This death was clearly signaled by the appearance early in 1969 of *Maximum Feasible Misunderstanding* by Daniel P. Moynihan, President Nixon's special advisor on urban affairs. Moynihan's book suggests clearly that not only the Community Action Program, which is its special focus, but indeed all of the attempts made by government officials and social scientists under the heading of the "war on poverty" were futile and misguided at best. The burial was completed by the appointment as OEO director of a conservative Republican congressman who during his career in the House consistently voted against appropriations for the Office of Economic Opportunity.

In spite of Moynihan's attack on community action and the general concept of poor communities organizing themselves, the last five years have also been characterized by the development and refinement of the concept of Black Power and its concomitant, community control. Black Power itself remains somewhat vague, being advocated by people as far apart politically as Stokely Carmichael and Whitney Young, Jr. At a minimum, however, Black Power applied to urban life in America clearly implies the control of community institutions, economic, political and social, in urban black communities. It is interesting to note that both Carmichael and Young supported, for example, the attempts of New York City communities to gain control over the public schools within them. It is the fundamental assumption of this chapter and indeed of the entire book that community control of urban institutions in predominantly black communities is absolutely essential for any serious change in the desperate plight of urban blacks. The following comments and suggestions are offered not as a cure-all for the problems of poverty in the entire nation nor as a blueprint for what must be done, but rather as a minimum program of development which would be a necessary but certainly not a sufficient cause for the eradication of urban poverty. Community control by itself is not a cure-all for the ills which plague American urban centers. The community control of inadequately financed social services, for example, is not likely to provide significant improvement. Nevertheless, a crucial and first step is to establish the principle that communities in urban America have the moral right to direct their collective destiny. And this moral right implies the right to operate their own businesses, political clubs and associations, educational institutions, and welfare services.

This chapter looks briefly at the possibilities in three important areas of urban life: economic development and manpower training, political development and neighborhood centers, and the community control of public schools. A "modest proposal" is then offered involving the community control of police forces.

Economic Development and Manpower Training

It is an obvious truism that the economic conditions in urban black communities are desperate. The percentage of people falling below the poverty line is higher in these communities than any other in the nation with the possible exception of rural Appalachia. Although black communities are economically isolated, they are not totally separated from the larger economy. Most of the income which does flow into the slums comes from three sources and illustrates the precarious nature of their economic existence. First of all jobs tend to come from the most backward sector of the economy and are characterized by low wages and seasonal fluctuations. Indeed a large portion of workers who are employed full time earn wages which still keep them below the poverty line. Another source of income is what some economists refer to as the "irregular" economy, partly legal and partly illegal, including numbers, dope and prostitution. Thirdly, income supplements from outside the urban poverty areas, both public and private, are a significant resource without which the population would probably not survive. Welfare payments are the largest and certainly the most controversial of this kind of income.

The most striking and sinister economic characteristic of black urban poverty areas is the continual drain of the limited resources available out of the area and into other sectors of the economy. Although difficult to measure, this economic drain has at least three aspects.

1) Human resources are weakened when slum neighborhoods expand and middle-class whites move out. This departure includes most of the professional personnel which could provide important personal and business services—doctors, dentists, lawyers, accountants, insurance agents and related professions—but which is not replaced. Human resources are also drained out through the education system. Those who are successful educationally, who seek higher income employment, by and large find this employment outside of an urban poverty area and tend to leave. These include clearly the best educated, capable, and imaginative young people, born and raised in urban slums.

2) The drain of capital is accomplished through investment policies of banks located in slum areas. A substantial portion of savings in these financial institutions is invested in business loans and mortgages elsewhere. Little comes back to support the local economy or to promote its development, even though the ownership of original savings remains with local residents. Probably the single largest flow of capital out of urban poverty areas takes place in the field of housing. Slum landlords who fail to maintain urban housing withdraw their capital while at the same time maintaining an income from it. Ultimately the property becomes worthless simply because of wear, tear, and neglect. But while it is being used up the owner has been getting his capital back and has been deriving a current income as well.

3) Income flows out of the urban poverty area in much the same way as capital and other resources. Earnings of residents are spent in stores owned from outside of their communities and in many cases staffed by employees from outside as well. The earnings and profits of these outside entrepreneurs are spent and invested elsewhere.

The most widely discussed attempt to deal with this dismal economic picture has been called by various names, including "black capitalism" and "community economic development." Regardless of criticisms of particular aspects, and there are many, it does seem to be the only possible approach for dealing effectively with the dire economic situation of urban black communities. The Congress of Racial Equality and its leader, Roy Innis, have been attempting to establish community development centers through federal legislation. These community corporations would coordinate economic development and community services. Through federal legislation, loans and certain tax incentives would be used to help these corporations run profit making enterprises, and then the earnings would be used to develop programs in health, welfare, and education. Innis describes how he envisions a community corporation would work.

> Suppose ... I am able with $100 million to create some kind of Harlem community corporation. And suppose the corporation obtains a contract to supply books, for instance, to the school system. You might object that the corporation does not have printing plants or publishing facilities. But the people who sell books now to the public school system in Cleveland and New York or anyplace else across this country are just middlemen who also do not have publishing facilities or printing presses. They buy them from someone else and sell them for a profit. In the corporation I have in mind profits derived from books and other materials used in the schools could be used to increase the income in the black community. Multiply the budgets for schools by the budgets for health and hospital services, sanitation and all the other urban services, the result is a massive amount of money that represents a guaranteed market and in economics a guaranteed market is the most important thing you can have. If you are selling to your own institutions you are able to determine who will get contracts and direct them to your own people.[2]

Manpower Training

In addition to turning around the economic flow which could be accomplished by the establishment of community development corporations, there is also a real and very important need for manpower training to provide occupational skills for residents of urban black areas. There is no reason why manpower training programs could not become an important part of the activity of community development corporations.

The first step in developing a comprehensive manpower development and job training program for an urban black com-

[2]Roy Innis, "Black Self-Determination," *New Generation*, Vol. 51, no. 3 (Summer, 1969), p. 21.

munity like Harlem is to look at the economic situation in New York and to try to make some projection of what the characteristics of the labor market are likely to be in the next few years. For New York City the following developments in manpower needs are predicted by the New York City Department of Labor for the decade of 1965 to 1975.

1. Professional, technical and kindred workers: including accountants, architects, clergymen, teachers, physicians, musicians, social welfare, and recreation workers. By far the greatest increase in employment in New York City is expected in this category. Some 75,000 to 80,000 more jobs will be available in 1970 than in 1960.

2. Clerical and kindred workers: including bookkeepers, cashiers, secretaries and stenographers, typists, postal carriers, and shipping clerks. The number of these positions will increase by 35,000 to 40,000 jobs.

3. Sales workers: including salesmen and sales clerks in retail and other than retail trade. Due to the increasing use of self-service techniques there will be an over-all decline in the number of persons in this field.

4. Skilled workers: including bakers, carpenters, electricians, mechanics and repair men, plumbers, tailors, and toolmakers. It is expected that there will be an increase of from 20,000 to 25,000 jobs in this category with the largest increases coming in the area of building trades craftsmen: carpenters, electricians, plumbers, plasterers, etc.

5. Semi-skilled and unskilled workers: including assembly line operators in most manufacturing fields, deliverymen, bus and taxi drivers, laundry and dry cleaning workers. The semi-skilled and unskilled workers (excluding service workers) are expected to decline by 70,000 to 80,000 jobs between 1965 and 1975. This is an area in which many black workers find employment.

6. Service occupations: including barbers, domestics, janitors, cooks, firemen, policemen, waiters, bartenders, and counter workers. It is expected that there will be an increase of 15,000 to 20,000 jobs from 1965 to 1975 in this category.[3] (*Youth in the Ghetto* reports that within this classification are employed

---

[3]*Manpower Outlook 1960-1970* (New York City Department of Labor, 1962).

26 per cent of Harlem males and 46 per cent of females in the labor force.)[4]

In addition to drawing out the implications of the above projection there are a series of additional steps which must be taken in developing a comprehensive manpower development and job training program for Harlem.

1. Outreach and recruitment. An effective program in Harlem not only must serve individuals who seek help in job training, but must find potentially employable people who have little or no motivation to look for employment services on their own. The neighborhood center concept described in the following section should be valuable in serving outreach and recruitment functions. Indigenous nonprofessional workers hired by the neighborhood centers should be able effectively to seek out and recruit local residents for a manpower and job training program.

2. Intake and evaluation procedures. The highest dropout rates in manpower development and job training programs usually occur within the first five days. Some of these dropouts can be traced to faulty intake procedures and bad evaluation. The purpose of the first interview should be to present the potential trainee with various educational and vocational alternatives. Formalized procedure should be avoided or kept to a minimum. It seems likely that a trained nonprofessional can conduct this interview as effectively as an outside professional. Once this interview has been completed the enrollee must of course be evaluated and in many cases tested to discover from which of the available programs he can profit. Great care should be taken at this stage to impress on an enrollee that he will not be dropped from a program on the basis of test results. Testing can be an anxiety provoking experience, particularly if the potential enrollee's skills in reading and writing are very low. Following the testing every attempt should be made to present the potential enrollee with alternatives which must of course be realistic in terms of the enrollee's background but should offer several possibilities for job training and future employment. Some provision must be made to permit an enrollee to change his vocational plan if it becomes apparent that this is desirable.

---

[4] *Youth in the Ghetto* (New York: HARYOU-ACT, 1964), p. 60.

An early decision to change vocational goals should not result in the enrollee's being dropped from the program. At this stage the question of supportive services must be considered. Many enrollees will require a variety of these if they are to be able to continue in a manpower program. Mothers of young children will need child-care services; heads of household may need financial assistance; transportation may be unavailable; certain health problems may have to be dealt with before the prospective enrollee can fully benefit from the training program. A careful consideration of these needs before the enrollee begins a training program should help to reduce the early dropout rate referred to above.

3. Prevocational Training. One of the crucial problems related to training programs that has been documented in Harlem and elsewhere is that many of the poor do not have the necessary skill level to benefit from training programs in most occupational areas. They may wish to become machine operators, or policemen but inability to read, write, and compute may prevent them from qualifying. To solve this problem an important element in a comprehensive manpower development and job training program must be prevocational training. In the section dealing with education we discuss adult basic education. It clearly has a significant role to play in job training since many adults in Harlem must receive adult basic education in reading, writing, arithmetic, and related skills before they can qualify for any training program. Many prospective enrollees will need instruction in how to apply for employment, what to expect during a job interview and how to complete application forms. Interest rates, withholding taxes, union participation, and social security may be totally outside their experience, but a knowledge of these becomes essential if the poor are to become employable. The New York City Board of Education has funded a Pre-Employment Training Program which it sponsors with Harlem Teams (formerly Associated Community Teams—ACT). PETP provided a combination of adult basic education and knowledge about the world of work. It had moderate success but served only young people from the ages of seventeen to twenty-one, and enrolled only a maximum of 250 in a twenty-week course. This kind of program could well be made

available to Harlem adults as well as young people, of course, on a much larger scale.

4. Vocational Training. Vocational training is clearly the heart of any manpower development program although it cannot be successful without the steps and considerations outlined above. There are two main types of vocational training. The first, institutional training, provided in classrooms or workshops, can be carried out by vocational schools, but can also be provided by neighborhood training centers or prospective employers. The second type, on-the-job training, relies heavily on learning by doing and by supervised experience. Occasionally employers have been guilty of exploiting trainees in these on-the-job training programs by providing little or no training. Follow-up support to on-the-job training sites should be thorough and if there is any indication that an employer is just working a trainee and not training him, that employer should be dropped from the program. What kind of training program should be offered in central Harlem? Based on the projected labor market outlined here the following appear to be likely areas for future employment: building and construction, printing, auto mechanics, medical occupations (nurses aides to practical nurses), home appliance repair services, commercial appliance services, clerical occupations, and electronic data processing. There are many levels of jobs included in each of these broad occupational categories.

5. Placement. After completing their manpower training program enrollees frequently need assistance in finding the job opening best suited to their abilities, especially those individuals who have been unemployed for an extended period of time. The primary objective is obviously not merely to find the enrollee any job but rather to find one for which he has been trained, and wherever possible one which provides the possibility of upward mobility.

6. Follow-up. No manpower program can prepare an individual for all problems that he will face on his new job. Follow-up support should be available from the manpower program for a minimum of six months after the enrollee has completed his training. A trained nonprofessional worker can perform this job well. Follow-up visits might be scheduled weekly for the first six

weeks, every other week for the next six and at least once a month for the balance of the first six-month period. The employer as well as the employee should be visited at the work site and the employee's foreman might be consulted provided that this would not antagonize the employee. This follow-up program is expensive since it involves a considerable number of man-hours for each employee who has been through job training. Yet, it is absolutely essential for the success of a manpower development and job training program. It provides on the one hand a check on the usefulness of the job training provided. Are the right skills being taught? Are there other skill areas needed by the employee in which he has received no instruction? Even more important it is necessary to assist the employee in adjusting to a work situation. There are likely to be a number of problems connected with this adjustment, particularly if an employee has been unemployed for a considerable length of time or if this is his or her first job.

7. Job Development. In addition to training and placing the poor in existing jobs a comprehensive manpower and job training program must concern itself with job development. This development may range all the way from obtaining changes in entrance requirements and qualifications for certain positions to actually encouraging the creation of new job categories for which poor people can be trained. The new careers for the poor concept has been developed by Frank Riessman and Arthur Pearl. Here in Riessman's words is the rationale for creating a whole new field of non-professional careers.

> 1. It can potentially provide millions of new jobs and careers for the unemployed in social service positions which are not likely to be automated out of existence. The major job types include: expediters whose function is to link services and people more efficiently—to mediate between the client and public and private agencies; direct service agents such as homemakers, teacher aides, mental health aides; community organizers or neighborhood workers whose function is to involve the residents of the area in community planning and community action.
>
> 2. It can provide more, better and "closer" service for the poor; it can reach the unreached, serve as a two-way communication bridge between professionals and the poor. Nonprofessionals can do things professionals cannot as easily do: they can be more "subjective,"

involved, provide more direct intervention, advice, companionship—they can be models for the poor. The nonprofessional has a number of unique characteristics that contribute to his potential effectiveness: local "know how," style of life, and peership.

3. It can rehabilitate many of the poor themselves through meaningful employment. This is based on the "helper therapy" principle. People with a problem helping others with the same problem is an approach well known to group therapists. In fact, some people who do not seem to benefit from *receiving* help often profit indirectly when they are *giving* help. This may be the case in a wide variety of group "therapies," including Synanon (for drug addicts), SCORE (Charles Slack's program for delinquents), Recovery Incorporated (for psychologically disturbed people), and Alcoholics Anonymous. The "helper therapy" principle has at least two important implications for the indigenous nonprofessional of lower socio-economic background: since many of the nonprofessionals recruited for anti-poverty programs will be school dropouts, former delinquents, long-term ADC mothers and the like, it seems quite probable that placing them in a helping role will be highly therapeutic for them; as the nonprofessionals benefit personally from their helping roles they should become more effective as workers and thus provide better help. Such a cycle could be an important positive force in a depressed community.

4. It can help make the professionals' role definitions more flexible, creating an alliance and unity between professionals and nonprofessionals which will allow the professionals more fully to play their technical roles. In addition, it can stimulate the development of new creative professional roles as trainers, teachers, and program planners. The "objectivity" of the professional combined with the "subjectivity" of the nonprofessional can provide a new complementary unity of service.[5]

It is important to note that Riessman is speaking of "new careers for the poor" not just in poverty programs but in positions which would be a permanent part of the helping professions. Anyone who has visited the hospitals, schools or any social agencies in Harlem should be aware of the great need for the kind of assistance which Riessman describes. Job development in this area might be a significant key to solving the unemployment problem in Harlem and other black communities.

[5] Frank Riessman, "The Helper Therapy Principle," *Social Work*, Vol. 10 (April, 1965), pp. 95-96.

Political Development—The Neighborhood Center

For purposes of analysis it is probably useful to separate problems of economic development from those of politics. But in fact, the two go hand in hand and from the perspective of the urban black resident they are inseparable. Without political community organization it would be impossible to operate anything like the economic community development corporations. Without political instruments reaching out into local neighborhoods, the problem of apportioning economic assets would be impossible to solve.

At the heart of any program for fundamental change in an economically depressed, segregated community such as Harlem must be a theory and program of political organization. The poor must be brought together to learn of their rights, to learn how to demand them, to decide on their own policies and programs, and eventually to take power in directing their own community's future. While almost all practitioners and probably most poor people would agree on this goal for a particular community, the methods for achieving it do not receive unanimous endorsement and in some cases flatly contradict one another.

The method of mobilizing the poor developed by Saul Alinsky, former University of Chicago criminologist, is one which has been used with considerable effectiveness in several poor communities, most notably Woodlawn in Chicago. The Woodlawn Organization is a federation of some eighty-five community groups including thirteen churches and three business associations. Alinsky's method is frankly to build on certain widely held grievances which exist in a poor community. He views with considerable disdain the more traditional community organization approach which has been used by social workers in many communities. Alinsky thinks of himself as an agitator and uses the same techniques as labor organizers used when first creating American labor unions: boycott, picket, sit-ins, and threat of bloc voting. He speaks of the problems of the poor in terms of power: "The problem is that the underprivileged have no power over their lives and they know it. They want bread and opportunity; instead they're offered consolation, adjustment, arts and crafts, fun and games. No wonder they fail to respond. That's like prescribing aspirin to cure cancer. Show them how to get the power to achieve what *they* want, not what somebody else thinks is sufficient for them, and they'll uplift their community themselves."[6]

Alinsky is now operating or planning to operate in a number of cities including Rochester and Buffalo, New York. Alinsky's method of operation once he is asked into a community, follows a fairly standard pattern:

> Organizers from Alinsky's Industrial Areas Foundation filter the neighborhood, asking questions, and, more important, listening in bars, at street corners, in stores, in people's homes—in short, wherever people are talking—to discover the residents' specific grievances;

> At the same time, the organizers try to spot the individuals and the groups on which people seem to lean for advice or to which they go for help: a barber, a minister, a mailman, a restaurant owner, etc.— the "indigenous" leaders;

> The organizers get these leaders together, discuss the irritations, frustrations, and problems animating the neighborhood, and suggest the ways in which power might be used to ameliorate or solve them;

> A demonstration or series of demonstrations are put on to show how power can be used. These may take a variety of forms: a rent strike against slum landlords, a clean-up campaign against a notorious trouble spot, etc. What is crucial is that meetings and talk, the bedrock on which middle class organizations founder, are avoided; the emphasis is on action, and on action that can lead to visible results.[7]

A considerably different approach to the question of community development is the one outlined in *Youth in the Ghetto, A Study of Consequences of Powerlessness*, produced by Harlem Youth Opportunities Unlimited in 1964. The basic program outlined in this proposal and later initiated by HARYOU is the establishment of local neighborhood boards. These boards consist of adults and youth, nonprofessionals and professionals, residents as well as those who work in the area and live elsewhere. The basic assumption underlying the proposals to create these neighborhood boards is that "there exist in the local neigh-

[6] Quoted in Patricia Cayo Sexton, *Spanish Harlem* (New York: Harper and Row, 1965), p. 129.

[7] Charles Silberman, *Crisis in Black and White* (New York: Random House, 1964), p. 327.

borhood actual or potential leaders both among the adults and youth." An additional assumption is that "local community leaders, many of whom will be without formal education and will lack the usual style and polish of social interaction could be stimulated to develop the confidence required and be able to utilize the skills of professionals in carrying out the mandate of the local boards, namely: 1) to develop social action, educational, and social welfare programs, 2) to conduct systematic community research, and 3) to inform local residents about available community resources."[8] It is clearly stated that the real test for these neighborhood boards would be their ability to involve those families and individuals who are not reached by already existing agencies and institutions.

This proposal for the creation of neighborhood boards is clearly more traditional than the Alinsky mobilization approach. However, it does provide for local initiative, participation, and to some extent control, which are among the ultimate objectives of Alinsky's method. In actual practice these neighborhood boards established by HARYOU have not become as effective as original drafters of the proposal envisioned. There are a number of reasons for this failure including local apathy, failure of professionals to give authority to non-professionals, and various personal and political conflicts within the Harlem community. The following section offers a modification of this neighborhood board concept which might help achieve the goals and objectives originally stated byHARYOU and also allow room for mobilization and political agitation by Harlem citizens.

The Neighborhood Center

Harlem may be a community but any plan to change it without making use of some smaller unit of organization seems doomed to failure. Therefore, at least ten neighborhood centers should be established in Harlem. These centers would be designed to meet a variety of needs for local residents. It might be useful here to look at how these neighborhood centers could help to solve four important problems which exist in a fragmented community.

[8]*Youth in the Ghetto*, p. 392.

1. People in a slum are frequently unaware of the many social agencies which exist to serve them. Many poor families who may be eligible for public assistance do not know whether or not they qualify. Many unemployed and underemployed people are not aware of local employment services or training programs that may exist. Sick people do not know about health facilities that are available. Many poor people with legal problems do not know about low cost or free legal services. The information that many poor people do have about existing agencies is often incomplete and possibly incorrect.

A basic function, then, of any neighborhood center would be to make people aware of agencies that exist to serve them and to make sure that Harlem uses every available resource in the "war on poverty." In creating this awareness the neighborhood centers would employ the techniques of outreach, referral, and follow-up. Outreach means that the workers in the neighborhood center must establish personal contact with neighborhood residents in their homes, their churches, their barber shops, their bars, and their streets. Local residents employed by the center as well as volunteers would be used for this purpose. This outreach would not only provide information for the poor but would in turn provide a line of communication to the neighborhood center through which the poor could express their needs and desires.

Referral, a standard social work concept, means that in those cases where the services needed cannot be provided by the neighborhood center itself, the individual will be referred for help to other public and private agencies. This referral must be more than the name and address of an impersonal office downtown. In many cases the staff in the neighborhood center must intercede on behalf of the local resident and assist him in a personal and direct way.

Follow-up means that in each case where a local resident has been referred for assistance, a staff member must make sure that effective service has been delivered. Follow-up then would require a careful system of record keeping. These records would also be helpful in evaluating the performance of the center and the performance of agencies to which residents are referred.

2. A second problem which confronts the poor in Harlem is that many offices, clinics, and training centers are located either

outside of Harlem itself or at a considerable distance from the resident's home. Poor people in general feel uneasy about venturing out of their own neighborhoods and into strange parts of the city. To solve this problem the neighborhood center would promote the decentralization of services and programs. This would be accomplished both by encouraging other private and public agencies to decentralize as well as by offering a variety of services through the center itself. There will obviously be difficulties with this concept of decentralization in Harlem. Many agencies would, however, decentralize if facilities were made available to them in the neighborhood center. Others might not be willing to open a complete local office but might perhaps attach one staff member to the center. A decentralized approach is part of the main thrust of the "war on poverty." Under certain circumstances it would be possible to use federal poverty money to pay the salaries of decentralized personnel from other agencies. To obtain these funds, however, there must be clear evidence that the other agency does not have money to accomplish the decentralization but is agreeable in principle.

Being poor does not represent a single problem. It means more than a simple lack of money and frequently poor people need assistance from a combination of social agencies. Unfortunately most agencies specialize in one kind of problem: unemployment, or health, or education, or public assistance. There is also a division of responsibility based on the level of government with federal, state, and local government agencies as well as a host of private agencies having similar programs in many areas. All of these services and programs must be brought together.

3. The neighborhood center can help provide coordination that is absolutely essential for a real attack on poverty. Through decentralization the center provides a single source of help for local residents. He no longer must visit a dozen offices. Coordination of course does not automatically follow decentralization, and there is unfortunately no detailed blueprint available. The following guidelines, however, should prove helpful. Everyone in the center, regardless of who pays his salary, should be administratively responsible to the director of the neighborhood center. All personnel should participate in staff training programs and be fully aware of the prevailing philosophy of the center. Refer-

rals within the center should be followed up as intensively as referrals to outside social agencies. A neighborhood center should be flexible enough to deal with almost any problem of poverty. Clearly expressed need on the part of local residents should be the important determining factor.

4. We have been concerned with the reorganization of existing services by neighborhood centers. However, there is an additional problem which cannot be solved through reorganization. It is that existing services in many areas are completely inadequate. In some cases quality is good but there is simply not enough of it. In other cases the service is so mishandled that it simply does not meet the real needs of the poor. A list of existing services which are inadequate in Harlem would include programs in almost every area, such as housing standards and code enforcement, job training programs, street cleaning, recreation facilities.

To some extent the decentralization and coordination of services described above should result in improving both quality and quantity in services available, but this will very likely still not do the job. Neighborhood people will have to organize themselves to demand additional services and undertake action to make their demands seen and heard by those in the power structure. This demanding may take the form of picketing, boycotting, or sitting or lying in. The effective use of these techniques requires the mobilization of neighborhood residents and training in action techniques. Politics looms large when dealing with mobilization, but certainly the legitimate expression of complaints, needs, and desires by the poor is a central part of the philosophy of the "war on poverty." The neighborhood center can play an important role in supporting the genuine neighborhood sentiment and in making effective the residents' demands for different and additional services and programs.

The staff of a neighborhood center should be made up of a very small number of professionals and a relatively large number of resident workers. Wherever possible the professionals themselves should be local residents. Local non-professional workers can be used in a variety of ways. After a carefully worked out training program these non-professionals should be extremely effective in outreach work; referral and follow-up work, getting people to agencies and making sure that they get service they need; as spokesmen for people in the neighborhood in dealings with a variety of institutions in the community including the neighborhood center itself; and as clerical staff and administrative assistants. Professionals assigned to neighborhood centers must be made to understand the importance of working with local nonprofessional people. Their role in most cases should be that of consultant. They should advise and offer alternatives but they should not be policy makers. Governing policy boards for each center should consist primarily of poor residents of the neighborhood. It should not be made up of professional experts from the various service fields offered by the neighborhood center. This kind of maximum participation by the poor can be extremely important in making the operation of the center acceptable.

This brief outline of the neighborhood center concept is not meant to be rigid and predetermined. Flexibility is extremely important since the problems of poverty exist under different circumstances and manifest themselves in many ways. Moreover, the neighborhood center approach can provide for the mobilization of the poor across neighborhood boundaries for more general political and social demands.

Community Control of Schools

Certainly more public attention and public feeling have been aroused by the conflict over community control of urban schools than any other aspect of this issue. Ocean Hill-Brownsville in Brooklyn and Intermediate School 201 in East Harlem have become crisis points of considerable magnitude. Although the most serious conflicts have taken place in New York City, some movement toward community control of urban schools has occurred in other metropolitan centers. Community control advocates in black neighborhoods have focused their attention on the schools for obvious reasons.

First of all, they are visible institutions in local communities which take their orders from sources outside the community. They are, of course, as many other social service institutions, staffed by outsiders. Perhaps most importantly, because of their function they involve practically the entire youth of the community. It is also important to note that the failure of schools is more easily documented than the failure of other social institutions such as hospitals or welfare. It is quite easy to show that the educational attainment levels of urban black youngsters are considerably below both national norms and the norms for their cities. Schools are expected to involve the public in their programs and are required to maintain some kind of relationship with the parents of the youngsters they serve. For all these reasons, then, schools have received the most concentrated attack by those favoring community control. Over the strong opposition of the United Federation of Teachers, the public school administrators, and most of the professional educationists in the New York City area, the New York State Legislature in 1969 passed legislation which at least made a beginning toward providing a legal framework for increased community power in the operation of local schools. Although the bill has been described by many community control advocates as a victory for conservative forces, it does, nevertheless, represent a first step which did not satisfy the anti-community control forces.

With this beginning the authors believe it is important that advocates of community control, while concentrating their efforts on the political process of obtaining more control, must begin to consider the kinds of institutional and curriculum changes suggested here for Harlem but applicable to other urban black communities.

Education in Harlem

There seems to be little disagreement among observers that the schools of New York City have failed miserably to provide their stated objective of quality integrated education. The youth of Harlem attend, in almost all cases, segregated and inferior schools and Harlem residents are not unaware of this. Parents of youngsters who were in PUL's day and resident camps were asked to identify the single most important problem facing Harlem. Choosing from a list which included lack of economic opportunity, narcotics addiction, police brutality, and juvenile delinquency, a majority selected bad schools. There is plenty of evidence to support this choice. Here is Kenneth Clark's summary of New York City Board of Education data as reported in his book, *Dark Ghetto:*

> In the third grade Harlem pupils are one year behind the achievement levels (in reading and arithmetic) of New York City pupils. By the sixth grade they have fallen nearly two years behind; and by the eighth grade they are about two and one half years behind New York City levels and three years behind students in the nation as a whole.[9]

Although there is a general agreement about the failure of educational institutions in Harlem there is much less agreement about the causes. The proposals made in this section for improving the educational picture in Harlem can be supported by educators and scholars who may still disagree on the causes for this failure.

The concept of education includes activities and programs that fall outside of the regular grades one through twelve, nine to four, September to June school year. The following three programs are of this nature.

Pre-School Education

Headstart as a national program of pre-school education has received considerable attention in the general press and a good deal of support from national leaders including the President of the United States. The rationale for this program is basically a simple one, although some parts of it are controversial. The designers of Headstart believe that poor youngsters, or more specifically those that can be described as "culturally deprived," are not as well equipped as are middle-class youngsters to learn in school. This lack of certain kinds of experience and support in the home is the major cause of the discrepancy in performance on school tests as reported by Clark above. Although Clark himself has questioned the "cult of cultural deprivation" as he puts it, he along with almost all scholars and educators supports the idea of a Headstart program. In operation the Headstart program is designed to be in most cases an eight-week summer pre-school experience for youngsters who will be entering either kindergarten or first grade in the fall. One basic question which must be asked about this summer experience: Is eight weeks

[9] Kenneth Clark, *Dark Ghetto* (New York: Harper and Row, 1965), p. 121.

long enough to do the job properly? The evidence is not yet in, but the first indications are that an eight-week Headstart program is not likely to make significant differences in the school achievement of a poor youngster. The failure of the summer Headstart program appears not to be due to any inherent weakness in the program itself but rather to the fact that the large classes and poor teaching in the public schools soon wash out the headstart possessed by the youngsters at the end of the summer program. If this preliminary indication is borne out by further evidence, the decision must then be made either to drop the Headstart concept or modify it so that it will in fact make a difference in later educational achievement. A few Headstart programs are operating on a year-round basis, and it seems to the authors of this book that the year-round approach to pre-school educational experience makes a good deal more sense. Our proposal for Harlem youngsters then is a year-round educational effort to provide the opportunity for pre-school experience for all of the three-, four- and five-year-old youngsters in Harlem. This would clearly be a massive undertaking and one that would require considerable additional federal funds. It is also one that would have to be developed outside of the public school system which has neither the staff nor the physical facilities to develop it and outside of the Department of Welfare's Day Care program which has some one hundred centers throughout New York City providing full day care for only 5,000 children of poor working mothers. Initially, at least in the development of such a program, it will be impossible to provide this service for all Harlem children. Preference must then be given to children from no- and one-parent homes, aid to dependent children families, and those with parents who are suffering from serious economic and physical disabilities. This pre-school program would be physically located in existing social agencies, churches, and housing projects. It is unlikely that many new facilities would have to be built.

After-School Centers

A year-round program of pre-school activities should certainly help Harlem children to better academic achievement. But what of the youngster already in school? It would be both immoral and foolish to write them off as an educational loss. One important method of providing assistance for school age youngsters would be through the establishment of after-school remedial centers in Harlem. The goals of these after-school centers would be to assist elementary school children in reading, writing, arithmetic, and speech. These basic skills are essential for other kinds of learning. For those centers serving Harlem high school students, more advanced remedial work must be provided in mathematics, science, social studies, and English composition. Of approximately 35,000 elementary and junior high school students in Harlem, at least half would seem to require remedial assistance. These centers also then represent a massive educational effort.

It seems appropriate at this point to say a few words about the use of volunteers in educational programs. On a smaller scale in Harlem and other poor communities throughout the country, volunteers have been effectively used in tutorial remedial programs such as the one we are suggesting here. It is certainly appropriate wherever possible to make use of community resources including volunteers. Volunteer tutors, of course, require closer supervision and certainly a training period before they can be fully effective. Although it would be unrealistic to expect an entire remedial program designed to serve some 18,000 youngsters to be manned by volunteers, they can certainly make an important contribution in both the pre-school program and the after-school centers. The use of the poor themselves, parents, other adults and older youth in these educational efforts will be spelled out in more detail later in the chapter.

Adult Basic Education

If there is any group which is consistently overlooked in thinking about educational problems of the poor, it is that proportion of the adult population which can be classified as functionally illiterate. There are sixteen million illiterates in the United States, eleven million of whom fall into the category of extreme poverty. Nearly two and a quarter million of the unemployed who are actively seeking employment are illiterate adults. As might be expected, both underemployment and low earnings are characteristic of those who are employed. The por-

portion of illiterate adults found in minority groups, particularly black, is high. The argument for supporting a massive program of basic adult education in Harlem is as that for the after-school centers, namely that it is both foolish and immoral to sacrifice the lives of adults and concentrate all educational efforts on children and youth. Adult Basic Education as the title says is concerned with very basic goals. They can be stated as follows: *reading*—an ability to read and comprehend what is read at a level equivalent to at least an average eighth grade pupil; *writing*—an ability to complete applications and other employment forms clearly and legibly, to compose simple letters and to make out orders; *arithmetic*—the mastery of basic addition, subtraction, multiplication, and division and the understanding of the practical application of these skills, such as the reading of scales, or the use of units of measurement and common decimals and fractions; *speech*—an ability to understand instructions and be understood in normal employment and other conventional situations. In those programs where high school equivalency is the goal, instruction must also be included in citizenship to provide knowledge equivalent to the level achieved in high school civics instruction. It can be seen from these goals that an adult basic education program is not synonymous with employment training or retraining, but in most cases is a prerequisite for it. It is hard to imagine an adult without the skills outlined above benefiting from a training program in any occupational area. For Harlem, then, a massive program of adult basic education is recommended which must include the identification of adult functional illiterates, a campaign to persuade them to participate in the program and, perhaps most important, a carefully worked out system of counseling and referral so that when the goals stated above have been achieved by an adult in the Harlem community he will be directed to either a job training program, a job itself, or further educational programs of some kind. It would seriously reduce the effectiveness of an adult basic education program if this guidance and referral system were not established. The program must make, and be seen to make, a difference in the life of those people who participate in it. If this difference is not evident, it is almost inevitable that the program will die quickly.

The Public Schools

So far in this discussion of educational problems nothing has been said about the public school system itself. No comprehensive revamping of the educational effort in a slum community like Harlem would amount to very much without serious attention to the on-going school program itself. From the Clark quotation at the beginning of this section it is clear that the schools in Harlem have failed. There seem to be two general views of the reasons for this failure. One view holds that the main fault of this failure lies with the children themselves and with the environment of the community. The young people come lacking certain skills, do not receive the proper support or encouragement at home, and thus fail. An opposite view begins with the hypothesis that the main reasons for educational failure lie within the school itself as a social institution in its failure to understand and utilize the talents which poor children have and in its expectation of and emphasis on certain middle-class patterns of behavior. Although not denying the importance of environmental influence on children as well as teachers and school administrators, the authors believe that the most productive approach is that which concentrates on changes in the organization and curriculum in schools, on the training of teachers, and on providing auxiliary staff to assist professional educators in their work. From this viewpoint then, several proposals are made for educational changes which will improve the effectiveness of public schools in Harlem.

Curriculum

One of the perennial problems in designing effective curricula for public schools in New York City is the deadening bureaucratic emphasis on uniformity. Students on the same grade level in all classes in all schools are required to be learning the same material at the same time. This kind of "equality" has stifled individual teachers and school administrators in their attempts to be creative. One of the obvious advantages of real community control of schools would be the development of variety and divergence in curricula, particularly in the early elementary grades. This flexibility should extend even within schools so that a school could have an approach to learning which would stress early learning and readiness, an approach which would stress an experience related program of teaching language and reading while another teacher might offer the regular programs of reading and arithmetic. Mounting evidence indicates the importance of the first years of learning. It is therefore recommended that the class size of the first three years be greatly reduced, preferably to less than twenty students per teacher. Furthermore, the emphasis in Harlem schools should be in the first three years on the development of each child with careful evaluation of his progress toward clear-cut tasks and goals. In these years the child should not be failed or expected to repeat a grade or year. If this ungraded approach for the first three years proves successful, it may well be applied in the fourth, fifth, and sixth years as well. (Note: For an expanded discussion of the non-graded elementary school, see Goodlad, J. I. and Anderson, R. H., *The Non-Graded Elementary School* [New York: Harcourt, Brace and World, Inc., 1963].)

Teachers in Harlem Schools

The importance of providing well-trained and highly motivated teachers for Harlem schools cannot be overstated. Even with bad school organization, ineffectual administration and a poor community, effective teachers can make a difference. Their recruitment and training for Harlem schools must be central for any program of revamping. Although it can never be the direct responsibility of community residents to train teachers, they should be aware of the failures and general ineffectual attempts in this area. Vernon F. Haubrich has developed a penetrating series of questions which could well be asked by the citizens of Harlem of those responsible for training teachers for their classrooms.

> 1. Is the faculty of the college which is preparing teachers involved in the disadvantaged schools? If the faculty is active in these schools—consulting, supervising student teachers, conducting research—students will be reassured that the need is genuine, not pedantic. If the faculty wants the program to go, it must become involved.
> 2. Does the curriculum of the preparing institution reflect the necessary modifications in the areas of cultural anthropology, sociology, psychology, and factors of political and historical relevancies? As an

example, one cannot teach Puerto Rican or Negro youths without knowing a great deal of their history and their culture.

3. Are relevant specialists from the school district and the college utilized to afford the prospective teacher the necessary skills and procedures in teaching the disadvantaged? Here is where the team approach has meaning for prospective teachers.

4. Do prospective elementary and secondary teachers have an understanding of the skills involved in teaching reading, and do they fully understand that in many schools serving disadvantaged areas all teachers are, in some measure, reading teachers? Has the college provided the necessary background and the school the opportunity to test these skills?

5. Are procedures established for the careful induction of the prospective teacher during his first few days in the school?

6. Does the college have a continuing program within these schools so that the young teacher does not feel abandoned during his first years of teaching?

7. Is there an effective understanding by the prospective teacher of the family, neighborhood, and peer group in the particular area where he is about to teach? Are field trips made to community agencies to reinforce his understanding?

8. Are the student teachers volunteers? Is there a provision made that, wherever possible, the student teacher may remain as a regular teacher in the school where the student teaching was completed?

9. Do the school and college provide the necessary recognition to teachers for service in disadvantaged areas?[10]

Unhappily the answer to virtually all of these questions when asked about teacher education for Harlem schools is "No." With these questions turned into directing guidelines, an effective program of teacher education can be designed. Beyond a design for providing effective teachers there should be emphasized the importance of the attitude and expectation which educators hold concerning black and "culturally deprived" youngsters in general. The best training in the world can make little difference if the teacher and school administrator do not believe youngsters can learn. This problem of teacher attitude and expectation is a particularly difficult one for which there seems to be no specific educational program. One can assume, however, that with in-

[10]From *The Reading Teacher* (March, 1965), pp. 499-505. "The Culturally Disadvantaged and Teacher Education," by Vernon F. Haubrich, Chariman, Department of Education, Teachers College, Columbia University.

creased knowledge of minority groups and increased interaction with the community in which the school is located, the expectation that black youngsters can learn will become a part of the psychological equipment of all Harlem teachers.

Nonprofessionals in Education

One of the most promising developments in thinking about education in slum areas is the growing interest in the role of the nonprofessional in educational work. Teacher aides have, of course, existed for a long time and are presently working in hundred of schools across the country. Recent plans have concentrated on employing the poor local community resident as an aide in a school in his or her own community. We believe this idea has exciting possibilities for Harlem schools. Three assumptions about this program are basic: 1) The aide who comes from the pupil's own community has a knowledge of the child's background. The aide will be able to clarify much that puzzles the child when he finds that the teacher and school expect him to know what is unfamiliar or to follow a pattern of behavior that may be quite different from that demanded of him at home. 2) An aide who knows the child's home and community can help to explain the child and his background to a teacher who may come from a quite different background. 3) The aide can help interpretation and communication between home and school, and assist parents to help their children. They can also help both parents and school officials realize the need for cooperation between the school and the home. In addition to these three basic assumptions, it is clear that the use of effective teacher aides can free teachers from routine jobs so that they can use their professional skills more effectively. Pupils may be divided into smaller groups with each one in turn receiving more specialized attention.

Besides these educational purposes for the use of local community teacher aides, there is another obvious economic reason for this program. By training underemployed or unemployed men and women to perform useful, needed services in the schools, kindergartens, nurseries and day-care centers, both the community and the children will benefit. In the cases where parents serve as aides in the school, they may well gain insight into the behavior of their own children and their educational needs, and hence become better parents.

It is extremely important that low income persons who may themselves have had bad experiences in schools be carefully trained for positions as school aides. A good training program must be a joint program training aides together with teachers and administrators. For an aide an effective training program should include instruction in child development, in methods and equipment used in teaching and caring for children, together with opportunities to observe and work with teachers and children in the classroom. For teachers and administrators instruction should be provided on the cultural background and problems of minority groups, particularly blacks in the case of Harlem. In addition to a pre-service training program which would most likely be given in the summer, there should also be a follow-up in-service training course, involving workshops and conferences for aides and teachers jointly.

A Modest Proposal—Community Control of the Police

No relationship in urban America today has received as much comment, discussion, analysis and heated debate as the relationship between urban police forces and black communities. The police represent once again an outside institution over which local black communities have absolutely no power. The two closely related factors of racial prejudice and brutality on the part of police provide the immediate motive for this proposal. However, it would also be possible to make a case for the local community control of police without evidence of police misconduct. Some figures on the extent of both prejudice and police brutality are available from studies by the National Crime Commission. These figures paint a very grim picture.

In Washington, D.C., the figures on racial prejudice of white officers serving in predominantly black precincts are as follows: 86 per cent of the white officers were found to be either "prejudiced" or "highly prejudiced" against blacks, the very people whom they are supposed to serve. Of that 86 per cent, 40 per cent were considered prejudiced and 46 per cent highly prejudiced, which is defined as those who referred to blacks in sub-human terms, suggested extreme solutions for our racial problems, or made other very extreme statements. Some examples of such statements cited in the study are "These scum aren't people; they're animals in a jungle." Or, "Hitler had the right idea. We oughta' gas these niggers—they're ruining the country."[1]

While accompanying officers during 850 eight-hour patrols in a number of major cities, National Crime Commission observers reported twenty instances in which "officers used force when none was clearly required or where its use was clearly excessive."[2] The instances cited by the Crime Commission included general beating, and kicking and hitting in the groin of men who were not always black but almost always poor. Assuming that Washington, D.C., is an average city in terms of police brutality, these figures mean that over fifteen acts of brutality would occur in Washington every day and about 5,000 a year. These facts clearly indicate that some fundamental change in the relationship between police and black communities is essential. While we do not suggest that institutional changes would reduce prejudice, we would argue that the proposal outlined below could affect behavior.

Citizens Precinct Review Boards

Citizens Precinct Review Boards should be established to consist of seven members: five private citizens elected by the community; one patrolman, a low-ranking officer in the precinct elected by the community; and one youth between the ages of sixteen and twenty-one elected by the community. (This is not to suggest that other members of the five private citizens category could not also fall into this age range.)

This Citizens Precinct Review Board should have the following powers:

1) To select from a Civil Service register the precinct captain and other top precinct officials. Using the register would assure that no unqualified officers would be appointed. Such a voice in selecting the high precinct police officials would certainly result

[1] *National Crime Commission Reports*, Field Surveys 3, Vol. 2, p. 133.

[2] *Task Force Report on the Police*, p. 182.

in precinct officers paying closer attention to the feelings and opinions of the community which are now almost totally neglected.

2) To hear all citizens' complaints against particular officers in the precinct; to recommend disciplinary action against such officers to the city-wide Citizens Police Personnel Board; and to require transfer out of the precinct of officers who are the object of particularly frequent or serious citizen complaints. Procedural safeguards would, of course, be provided for police officers as well as complaining citizens, particularly in the case of a hearing on a transfer of a police officer since such action would be final. The police department would then have the responsibility of reassigning the officer to another precinct or to a job involving less contact with the community.

3) To establish in consultation with precinct and central police department officials guidelines for personnel assignments and law enforcement policies in the precinct, particularly with regard to the enforcement of statutes regulating street conduct. Enforcement policies for serious crimes such as murder, theft, and robbery could certainly be set by the central police department headquarters. Community involvement would be essential, however, for the enforcement of such street conduct statutes as disorderly conduct, vagrancy, drunkenness, gambling, and juvenile delinquency. *These crimes are the major areas of police-community contact and police-community conflict.* Policemen have traditionally had broad discretion in enforcing these statutes and the largely unchecked exercise of this discretion results in uneven and racially discriminatory law enforcement.

Citizens Police Personnel Board

The city-wide board would be composed of the chairman of each of the precinct review boards and would sit in panels of five or seven as a quasi-judicial tribunal to hear and act on the recommendations for disciplinary action made by the precinct review boards. All cases would be presented by the board's own staff attorneys and investigators on behalf of complaining citizens. Police officers accused of misconduct would be represented by counsel provided without charge by the city government.

In conclusion it is important to note that there is nothing anti-police or anti-law and order about this proposal. This proposal in fact would directly attack one of the basic problems of law and order, which is that in urban black communities many citizens see the police as the enemy or as an occupying army enforcing the white man's laws. If the black community has some say over who the police are and how they apply and interpret the law, the police force may well get the community support and respect which it has been demanding.

Conclusion

What are the possibilities for the implementation of the programs outlined in this chapter? Certainly in the short run, over the next decade or two, the possibilities cannot be described as encouraging. The general right wing shift in American politics as evidenced by the election of Richard Nixon as President can in no way be interpreted as supporting the kinds of power redistribution and financial support required for the programs which have been advocated. The federal government apparently sees itself as caught between increasing demands of minority group citizens for an improved quality of life and opportunity for advancement and, probably more important, the unwillingness of the majority to provide the resources needed to offer such opportunities. Our large cities are clearly arenas in which this tragic conflict seems likely to be played out.

The United States has successfully landed men on the moon's surface, an achievement that involved highly trained workers, years of research and a financial investment of some thirty-five billion dollars. The decision to invest the brains and money needed to accomplish this task has apparently been a very popular one. It seems highly unlikely, however, that the investment of an equivalent amount of brains and money in solving the nation's urban problems would be equally popular. Yet it is hard to see how anything short of an investment of the magnitude of ten to fifteen billion dollars a year could do the job that is required. No one now can believe that the achievement of community control and black community power in America will be easy. If the future is bleak, as indeed it appears to be, it still seems to the authors of this book necessary to continue developing programs, pushing them politically and socially wherever possible, making strong and forthright demands for a better economic share from all levels of government, and most importantly to participate in the development of radical political alternatives on the national level.

If it is true that the resources and intellectual commitment are unlikely to come from our present political leaders, then new ones must be gotten. Political leaders sympathetic to the aspirations of urban blacks and indeed to the aspirations of all poor Americans, white or black, rural or urban, are unlikely to come out of the present two-party structure in American politics. The assassination of Robert Kennedy and the political eclipse of Eugene McCarthy may well have been the death knell of the possibility of radicalizing a major political party in the United States. Although it is not the task of this book to identify the membership of this new political movement, it would certainly include the poor; the growing number of disenchanted professionals; and youth, both in and out of universities. This political alignment, while not being identical with and perhaps not even including some members of the New Left in America, nevertheless must take some of its impetus from that movement. Christopher Lasch in *The Agony of the American Left*, while in many ways critical of the New Left, does suggest what may be the most crucial values of that political movement.

> It is true that the New Left has articulated values, derived for the most part from an indigenous tradition of radical populism, that might become the basis of a new socialism addressing itself to the needs of the twentieth century, not to those associated with the early stages of capital accumulation. In espousing decentralization, local control, and a generally antibureaucratic outlook, and by insisting that these values are the heart of radicalism, the New Left has shown American socialists the road they must follow. Until American socialism identifies itself with these values, it will have nothing to offer either to black people or to all those others whose suffering derives not merely from the private ownership of the means of production but from the dehumanizing effects of bureaucratic control.[13]

[13]Christopher Lasch, *The Agony of the New Left* (New York: Alfred A. Knopf, 1969), p. 211.

Index

Date Due